THE EARLY CHURCH FATHERS AS EDUCATORS

BY ELIAS MATSAGOURAS

An Excellent Study Book to Use with Church School Teachers.

A hermit with his disciple

The Early Church Fathers as Educators

by

Elias G. Matsagouras

To my wife Helen

Light and Life Publishing Co.
Minneapolis, Minnesota
Printed in the United States of America

Library of Congress Catalog Card Number 77-78601

Table of Contents

Abbreviations 7
Preface 9
Introduction 11
- I. Purpose of the Study
- II. History of Monasticism
  - A. The Origins of Monasticism
  - B. Evolution of the Monastic Spirit

Chapter I. Educational Activities in the Early Church . 19
- A. Hellenism-Christianity
- B. The Church's Stand with Regard to Classical Schools and Education
- C. Christian Education

Chapter II. Theoretical Ideas on the Main Questions of Education of the Early Fathers 33
- A. Heredity and Environment
- B. Divine Grace
- C. The Possibility of Education
- D. The Purpose of Monastic Education
- E. Ascetic Life as a Means for Monastic Education

Chapter III. Elder and Disciple 45
- A. Elder (Teacher)
- B. Disciple (Student)

Chapter IV. Teaching Methods and Discipline in Monastic Education 64

A. Teaching Methods
B. Discipline in the Monastic Educational System
Chapter V. Monks and Intellectual Culture 90
A. Their Attitude Towards Intellectual Culture
B. Monastic Schools
Epilogue.............................. 99
Appendix.............................. 102
Footnotes.............................. 108
Bibliography.............................. 122
A. Primary Sources
B. Secondary Sources

Abbreviations

A.N.F.	*Ante-Nicene Fathers*, ed. Al. Roberts (Buffalo; 1885 ff)
c.	circa (about)
d.	died
ed.	edition, editor, edited by
f.	and the following pages
fl.	to flourish
F.T.Ch.	*The Fathers of the Church*, ed. R. Deferrari (Washington: 1947 ff)
Ibid.	ibidem (in the same place)
Ms, MSS	manuscript(s)
ob.	obiit (died)
p.	page
P.G.	*Patrologia Graeca*, ed. J. P. Migne (Paris: 1857-1867)
P.L.	*Patrologia Latina*, ed. J. P. Migne (Paris: 1844-1855)
P.N.F.	*Nicene and Post-Nicene Fathers*, ed. P. Schaff (N. York: 1894 ff)
P.OR.	*Patrologia Orientalis*, ed. F. Graffin (Paris: 1903 ff)
S.Chr.	*Sources Chrétiennes*, ed. H. de Lubac Paris: 1941 ff)
St.	sanctus, saint
tr.	translation, translated by, translator
V.H.P.	*Vivliotheke Hellenon Pateron*, ed. Apostolike Diakonia tes Ekklesias tes Hellados (Athens-Greece: 1955 ff)

SIGNS:

† , to denote spurious works.

\+ , to denote works of doubtful authorship.

Preface

Among the many trends of the present time, an interest in the early patristic period, as well as in early monasticism, is noticeable. In a time of doctrinal vagueness and general uncertainty, not to say ambiguity, among modern Christians, the desire to go back to biblical and early patristic thought and sources is apparent. The experience of the stormy and unsteady early Christian centuries has a lot in common with our times.

Eastern monasticism, which has often been declared dead, shows again a remarkable revival both in the Holy Mountain in Greece and in Egypt. Many young and well-educated men and women opt for the religious life. The spiritual experience embodied in the rich tradition of the early Church, represented by such writers as the Cappadocian Fathers, Ephraem the Syrian, Macarius the Egyptian, Dionysios the Areopagite, Isaac of Nineveh, and John Climacus, just to mention a few, may satisfy those who would otherwise look to the religions of India, or the Far East, to satisfy their spiritual thirst.

The present study could be understood in such a context. Its main emphasis is upon the Early Church Fathers, including the hermits of the Egyptian deserts, whose works are being translated into new languages and studied by many eager students of that period. A somewhat surprising approach to the Desert Fathers is here taken. Who would regard them as educators? They certainly did not have a place in the educational system of their own times. In their austerity, they seem to have been anything but educators; yet their "sayings," and writings show that they were and still are educators in their own right. Here again, we find an example of the well-known fact that the Church, in all its other-worldliness, with all its eschatological thinking and longing, yet proves 'useful,' creative, and innovative in the spheres of culture, education, and art.

This study is of twofold interest. First, it is of interest to any student of the history of education and it really fills a gap in the existing literature. Secondly, it is a good introduction to some main issues of early Church history and to the history of monasticism and its surprising attitudes in several instances.

The Desert Fathers and their followers carried their message in an astonishing degree to all corners of the then civilized world and transformed both Church and culture and their influence is still felt. In these respects, this presentation might be of help to any student of both the early Church and of education.

Eric Segelberg
Dalhousie University
Halifax, N.S., Canada

Introduction

I. *Purpose of the Study*

This book is a study in the history of education. The history of education will not solve the problems of today, but it may help to achieve a better understanding of them and also it may serve to inspire its students towards more purposeful goals.

Since education is, among other things, the transmission of our intellectual and spiritual heritage, educators should know thoroughly the origins and the evolution of that heritage. This will enable them to study the origins and evolution of each problem and so to better understand it.

The main object of this study is education in the pre-Mediaeval Eastern Church, as this is illustrated in the educational activities and the writings of the Early Church Fathers. The era of the early Church has an important place in the history of Christianity, not only on the account of its spiritual standards, but also because it was a formative period for Christian thought and many Christian institutions.

This thought, as it was finally molded by the Early Church Fathers, came to be a decisive factor in the formation of Western civilization.[1] Many important features of it owe their origin, more or less directly, to patristic thought.

One of the channels via which Christianity has influenced Western civilization was monasticism. This appeared at the turn of the third century A.D., and soon became a dominant force in the life of the Church. Its influence began in the fourth century with St. Athanasius's work, *Vita Antonii* (*The Life of St. Antony*) and was prominent in Byzantine and Mediaeval cultures, as well as in the spiritual and intellectual life of Czarist Russia.[2]

The most celebrated figures of monasticism are known as the "Desert Fathers." They form a distinct and important group among the Fathers of the Church. In this study they receive special attention, since no systematic study has viewed them from an exclusively educational point of view. Their lives involved a continuous process of teaching and learning. Monasticism, and the whole Church in general, was a hard school with its own educational system and activities. Even though none of the Early Church Fathers—the Desert Fathers included—ever wrote an educational treatise, many educational ideas are scattered among their writings. These touched on such matters as the relative importance of heredity and environment, as they relate to spiritual and educational development, on teaching methods, and on the basic question of whether education is even possible.

The author searched and analyzed the extant early Christian literature, in order to illuminate such ideas. At the same time there was a need to study carefully the actions and the deeds of the Early Church Fathers, as a means of deducing which principles governed their educational endeavors.

II. *History of Monasticism*

A few comments concerning the history of Monasticism, including its origins, its spirit, and its development will be observed here as a necessary historical background to our theme.

A. *The Origins of Monasticism*

Monasticism was not a new kind of Christianity. It

sprang from the life of the early Church and its roots can be traced to the New Testament.

Christ spoke about those to whom sufficient strength had been given to make themselves eunuchs for the sake of the Kingdom of Heaven,[3] and St. Paul strongly recommended the unmarried life.[4] In other cases, Jesus suggested that his followers should live a life of poverty[5] and in his Epistles, Paul spoke in favor of an austere and devoted life[6] which the early Christians and monks tried to lead. The eschatological teaching of Jesus also led many people to reject the materialistic world. Moreover, the austere life of the prophets Elijah, Elisha and John the Baptist was a model which the early hermits claimed to emulate.[8]

The above mentioned Biblical references support two of the three monastic ideals, those of celibacy and poverty. The third was obedience, and it is equally well supported by biblical references, as shown in chapter II. Clement of Alexandria and his pupil Origen formed the essential elements of the ascetical theology, and made monasticism, as well as Christianity in general, more understandable to the Greek-speaking and Greek-thinking world.

The first hermits did not regard their lives as a new kind of Christianity, but rather they claimed to be returning to the Apostolic life.[9] Both St. Antony (251-356) and John Cassian (d. 433), the founder of western monasticism, regarded monastic life as a continuation of the Apostolic life.[10] Jerome, also writing sometime during the last years of the 4th Century, said that early Christians were used to living in an ascetic way, as the monks of his time did.[11]

Asceticism is a basic feature of monasticism in all places and in all periods. But the early Church, and the Eastern Orthodox Church to this day, perceived Christianity as a religion of sacrifice and ascetic life. Monasticism tried to fulfill the obligations which every Christian undertook with the vows he made at his baptism. The ascetic life of monks was not something "special" and "extra" but a fulfillment of the obligations which were common to all Christians. Thus, monasticism was regarded as a "second baptism" and its rites were based on the pattern of the rite of baptism.

Another characteristic of early Christianity was that the Church was a community of voluntary outcasts who had renounced the "world" and who considered themselves to be strangers in this world and citizens of the city to come.[12] Tertullian wrote: "nothing is more foreign to us than affairs of the state." Such was the official attitude and teaching of the early Church, which was accepted by a great number of Christians. When the Decian persecution began in 250 A.D., many Christians, obeying their bishops, went to the deserts where they continued their ascetic life under more rigorous conditions and they became the first Christian hermits. When the persecution was over some did not return to their cities but stayed in the deserts where they had found the ideal place for their spiritual exercises. The Decian persecution became the historical cause which made zealous Christians of the early Church familiar with the solitary life of the deserts and mountains.[14]

Later, when the age of persecution had passed, the strong desire for martyrdom as it is depicted in the Acts of the Martyrs, and the desire to engage in bloody battles of the faith, found an outlet in the self-immolation of the eremite. Monastic life then was considered to be "white martyrdom," i.e., unbloody martyrdom. Abba Macarius, pointing out the cell of two brothers said: "Come see the place of martyrdom of these lesser pilgrims."[15] This thought was also shared by St. Pachomius.[16]

With Constantine's Edict of Milan (A.D. 313), the Church was declared to be free and later under Theodosius I Christianity became the state religion of the Empire. Therefore, the spirit of martyrdom, which had originally brought many pagans to Christianity, gave place to worldly security. Many ardent souls became afraid that it was no longer possible to find salvation within the Church, which had become a secure, state-approved and partially secularized institution. To them monasticism was a safe means of completely devoting their lives to Christ.[17] The Church lowered its standards for its members, and began to follow along the road which the world had always followed, buying and selling, marrying and giving in marriage.[18] Thus, monasticism was an "Exodus," not so much from the world as from the world in the Church, "from court bishops who fought for richer seats, from people who bore the name of Christ, but who were still pagans at heart." [19]

The bishops, on the other hand, saw monasticism as an individualistic and separatist movement. However, in spite of the conflict between monasticism and the Church, the former never lost contact with the Church and its bishops. In his work *The Life of St. Antony*, St. Athanasius speaks of the great reverence St. Antony had for the Church officials. This had an impact on the evolution of the monastic movement. It encouraged its members to remain within the Church. Later, St. Basil (330-379), one of the most important monastic legislators, put monasticism in the service of the Church and society in general.[20] Finally, Canon Law imposed episcopal control over monasteries.[21]

Monasticism, however, besides being a reaction against the secularization of the Church, was also a reaction against the "intelligentsia," which entered the Church from the ranks of the Greek-educated believers. Moreover, there were other minor factors influencing the evolution of the monastic movement, namely some Greek philosophical trends[22] and certain Judaic elements, such traditions derived from the Qumran community, probably through Syrian Christianity, and the monastic life of the Egyptian Therapeutes. Finally, certain adverse socioeconomic conditions, and in general insecurity of life during late antiquity, might have been influences fostering the growth of monasticism, but they were by no means the main springs of it. The principal driving force of it was the Apostolic spirit, which, as mentioned above, was ascetic, prone to martyrdom, and full of eschatological agony. This spirit was transferred to the deserts and mountains of Egypt and the Middle East, where the life of the early Church was continued. This transfer gave birth to monasticism, whose contention was that "straight is the gate and narrow is the way, which leadeth unto life." [23]

B. *Evolution of the Monastic Spirit*

The life and work of the most illustrious men in monasticism, who played an important role in its formation, illustrate the evolution of the monastic ideal.

Antony, born in Egypt, is the first dominant figure in early monasticism. He is regarded as the "Father of Monasticism" although he was not the first in the field. There were others, the forerunners of Christian monasticism, who lived around the villages of Egypt from whom Antony received counsel.[24] These early ascetics did not know the "distant desert" but Antony went to the "inner desert." [25] After twenty years of solitary life, Antony came forth and undertook the task of directing the monks who were living around him. The Antonian organization would seem to have been very loose and entirely voluntary.

Famous for his virtues, Antony had a great influence upon his contemporaries and "persuaded many to choose the solitary life; and so henceforth there arose monasteries even in the mountains, and the desert was made a city by monks coming out from their own and enrolling themselves in the heavenly citizenship." [26] In the Egyptian deserts with the warm and rainless climate and the natural caves in the neighbouring mountains, thousands of monks found the ideal place for their practice. At the Mount of Nitria alone there were five thousand monks living different ways of life, as Palladius reports.[27]

The second step to a better organization was made by Pachomius (292-346), the father of cenobitism, who created his first monastery in Tabennisi in 323 A.D. By the time of his death, St. Pachomius had founded nine monasteries for men, and two for women, which counted their members in the tens of thousands. Pachomius is also the first monastic legislator. The fundamental idea of his Rule was to establish a common level of observance which might be reached by all the monks and then to encourage them to go beyond that minimum according to their desire and fortitude.[28]

After Pachomius, Shenoute of Atripe (348-466) was the most important figure of Egyptian cenobitism. He was an outstanding organizer and writer in Coptic. In his Rule, departing from Pachomius, he mentions a written monastic profession to be signed by the monks. These early cenobites had the character of a great army, and not of a family.

Basil (330-379), the father of eastern monasticism, with his Rule introduced the idea of small monasteries with thirty or forty monks, and he put a greater emphasis on education and culture.

The monastic movement spread all over the Middle East area. Monks were to be found in Coele Syria and Upper Syria according to the historian Sozomenus.[29] In all probability, Syrian monasticism is older than the Egyptian. By the end of the fourth century monasticism was established in Mount Sinai, Armenia, Persia and Mesopotamia. Hilarion, Eustathius and Chariton were pioneers in Palestine, while Jerome (340-420) and John Cassian made monasticism known and popular in the West. It soon became a part of the mediterranean landscape, and a powerful force in the hands of bishops against heretics, Jews and pagans. It influenced and troubled very much the life of late antiquity.[30]

The term monasticism, meaning the institution which establishes and regulates the ascetical and social conditions of religious life lived in common or in contemplative solitude, comes from the Greek word "monachos." This word originally meant "single," or "solitary" and later (perhaps at the beginning of the 4th century) it came to denote the "religious," i.e., the one who is living a monastic life, even in cases where he is living together with others. It seems that the first time the term "monachos," with the meaning "monk," was used is in *Vita Antonii* by Athanasius. Athanasius also uses the term "monastery," although it seems that in *Vita Antonii* this term should be understood in the strict etymological sense, i.e., a solitary cell and not as an abode of a group of monks, as it came to mean later. The terms "monk" and "monastery" occur in the *Apophthegmata*, and in Palladius, Basil and Nilus' writings. The term "moné," meaning "abode," was also used with reference to a cell or monastery. The life of a monk or nun was called "monastic life," and in Syriac "abbiloutha," meaning "sorrow."

The Latins used the Greek terms, i.e., "monachus," "monasterium," etc. In Chapter II of the present study, further terms referring to the monastic orders and offices are given.

This is a very brief review of early Christian monasticism. As an institution it has survived through the centuries and it is still viable in the modern world. It seems that it has a new urgency and thrill attracting those who are eager to impose a kind of reawakening upon our world. Monasticism now attracts people not only as a school of contemplation but also as a school of obedience and common life.[31]

Chapter I

Educational Activities in the Early Church

The theme of the present study is best comprehended within the context of the intellectual movements of the Christian Church during this period. Therefore, this chapter will aim at providing the necessary background by discussing three important questions:

A. Hellenism—Christianity, i.e., the Church's stand with regard to Greek thought and culture.

B. The Church's stand with regard to Classical schools and education.

C. Christian Education: its meaning, purpose and practice.

A. Hellenism—Christianity

The intellectual struggle between Christianity and the classical world that started in Athens with Paul's speech to the Athenians, continued through the next three or more centuries in such cities as Alexandria, where these two great forces confronted each other at that crossroad of history. To the early Church, classical thought was not just the armoury of pagan hostility towards Christianity, it also represented a debate within the very fibre of the Church, since many Christians who possessed a sound classical education wanted to use it for a better understanding of the new faith and paradoxically, even for a defence against pagan attacks. Thus, the early apologists had to speak Greek, both literally and metaphorically. They were addressing themselves to the Greek world and they had to express the new message in terms understood by their intellectual contemporaries. The rise of Christian theology and of Christian scholars who would attempt to unite Greek philosophy and Christian faith, was one result of this struggle. A brief survey here of the successive phases of this intellectual struggle will be given by presenting some of the representative schools of thought involved in this conflict.

I. Phase 1

Justin the Martyr (martyred 165 A.D.) is considered to be the noblest personality of the early literature, as well as the most important apologist of the second century. He is also deemed to be the originator of Christian philosophy. He tried to build a bridge between Greek philosophy and Christian faith by presenting the idea that Christ, the eternal Logos, had been active in human history, teaching and inspiring good and wise men everywhere, Greeks and Jews alike.[1] Thus, he wrote that the Platonic writings and the Bible expressed basically the same doctrine of God and the world, i.e., God is transcendent, nameless, incorporeal, impassible, and immutable. Furthermore, Justin praises Plato's teaching about the soul's kinship to God, its free will and the divine origins of the material world. Nevertheless, Justin also holds that the Bible is the complete divine revelation, and does not hesitate to reject Greek philosophical ideas that disagree with Biblical teaching. One example is his rejection of the Platonic doctrine of the transmigration of the soul. He had a great respect for most philosophers may contribute to the understanding of the Scrip-the life of reason to be Christians even though they previously had been thought to be atheists.[2] To some degree the Church accepted this idea. Plato, Socrates, Aristotle, Thucydides and other Greek thinkers were portrayed in Church vestibules together with the Old Testament prophets. Two other outstanding figures of the Church, Clement of Alexandria (160-215) and his great pupil Origen the Christian (185-254) continued Justin's line of thought. The former wrote that Plato was a zealous imitator of Moses,[3] and the latter that philosophers may contirubte to the understanding of the Scriptures. Starting from this basis, these two men rendered an important service to Christianity by legitimizing philosophy as a tool in the defence of Christian beliefs. Even though less educated believers were suspicious of philosophy, and reacted against it, Clement, a great teacher in the Church, used classical Greek literature for pedagogical purposes, while Origen, an outstanding scholar and original thinker, used the same literature in order to better understand and express Christian doctrine. Both Clement and Origen wanted to show that authentic Christianity was not obscurantism and that faith and knowledge are not incompatible. These were among the first to attempt a bridging of Christian faith and Greek philosophy.

Many of the later Fathers of the Church such as John of Damascus (7th-8th Century) and Nicholas Cabasilas (14th Century) continued to think along these same lines.

In comparing Christianity to Greek philosophy it can be said that Christianity had a universal application, since its solution to the problems of society and the individual were based on the moral nature of man, and faith, which is common to all men. Whereas Greek philosophy, accessible only to educated people, offered solutions only to a small intellectual elite.[5]

Classical education aimed at preparing man for the present life only. Christianity, however, saw man as the Son of God and the heir of the Kingdom of Heaven. Therefore, its concept of education was broader than the pagan, in that it had a new dimension, that of the Spirit.

II. Phase 2

The thought and the wisdom of the Alexandrian masters gave way to that of the Cappadocian and Antiochian Fathers who brought on the "golden century" of the Church. These Fathers were slightly reserved about classical "paideia," especially Chrysostom (347-411), the most important of the Antiochian Fathers who wrote: "I have long ago laid aside such fables [meaning philosophy] for one cannot spend all one's life in child's play."

The most important Cappadocian Fathers, Basil (330-379), Gregory of Nyssa (335-385) and Gregory of Nazianzus (330-390) were less reserved about philosophy and they successfully attempted to "translate" Christian faith into fundamental categories of Greek thought and language.[6] Although Basil warns us to be selective in studying classical works,[7] he cannot hide his admiration for classical learning. He wrote once to the celebrated pagan sophist, Libanius:

> I have read your speech and I have immensely admired it. O muses, O learning; O Athens; what do you not give to those who love you! What fruits do not they gather who spend even a short time with you? [8]

Gregory of Nyssa, one of the great Christian writers of the fourth century and a pillar of the eastern Church, stood both in the midst of Greek "pardeia" and at the same time above it, viewing the classical tradition as something foreign.[9] Their friend, Gregory of Nazianzus, one of the greatest orators of Christian antiquity, seems to have viewed the struggle of Greek philosophy for virtue, as related to the "Exodus" of Egypt. Comparing these three great Fathers, one can say that Gregory of Nazianzus was a lyrical poet with a noble soul, his bosom friend Basil, the ecumenical doctor, was a man of doctrine and action and Gregory of Nyssa, Basil's brother, was a mystical philosopher. These were the three Cappadocians whose contribution to theology and to the solution of the problem "Hellenism-Christianity," to the restoration of peace and to the expansion of the monastic ideal was such that it has had a lasting influence on the entire Church.[10]

However, all these Fathers were not able to defuse completely the arguments of those who were vigorously opposed to "secular philosophy" from the very beginning. Tertullian (active until 210-220) was such a one. He wrote: "What is there in common between Athens and Jerusalem, the Academy and the Church?" [11] The *Didascalia Apostolorum*, a third century document, also expresses strong opposition to it by saying:

> Have nothing to do with pagan books. . . . What connections can any Christian have with all the errors they contain? . . . The Bible not only provides for the supernatural life but for all cultural needs too . . . all these outlandish books . . . must be hurled away.[12]

At this time, Greek literature was certainly not a dead mythology, but rather the vehicle of paganism, the state religion, against which Christianity had to struggle. This therefore justifies to some extent such powerful opposition, and at the same time it shows how praiseworthy the effort of the Fathers was to couple classical beauty with Christian truth.

In sum, the early Church thinkers understood Christianity as a religion with ecumenical dimensions and realized that it had to be converted to some extent to the culture and outlook of late antiquity, before it was possible for it to convert the Greco-Roman world. Thus, the Church, while Christianizing the Greek-speaking and Greek-thinking world, itself became Hellenized to some extent. The first step which Christianity took towards Hellenism was the use of the Greek language. This was followed by the adoption of several philosophical ideas from Plato, Aristotle and the Stoics, which, under the shield of Christianity often acquired a new meaning. When "unchristianized" Greek thought entered the Church it led to the creation of heresies. Tertullian wrote: "Indeed heresies are themselves instigated by philosophy." [13]

B. The Church's Stand with Regard to Classical Schools and Education

It is clear from what has been said that the Fathers of the early Church to some extent recognized the usefulness of classical philosophy and culture, and also the need for "worldly" (non-religious) knowledge. This kind of knowledge was given only by secular schools, which were clearly pagan in character, both with regard to curriculum and structure. Surprisingly, the post-Apostolic Church, with few exceptions, did not make any serious effort to establish her own schools to teach her own children literature and other "secular" subjects, even though it had the example of the Jews who had organized their own schools.[14] E. J. Power, trying to explain why the Church did not establish her own schools, says that she had neither the time, nor energy, nor skill to supervise them.[15] Such an argument is not very convincing and the question remains open to dispute. The absence of Christian schools created a two-pronged dilemma:

I. Should young Christians attend pagan schools with the possible risk of being influenced by the school and losing their faith?

II. Should Christians be allowed by the Church to teach at pagan schools?

I. To the first question the majority of parents anwered in the affirmative. They sent their children to secular schools, after making them aware of the "proffered poison." Even the austere Tertullian approved of this. But Tertullian and later Chrysostom, placed on the shoulders of the parents the stern obligation of making their own Christian education so strong that pagan literature could not have any effect upon young Christians. Having this in mind, Christians continued to accept and use the classical schools, without accepting the culture it supported. With the appearance of monastic schools, parents had an alternate way in which to educate their children without risking their children's faith. Chrysostom advises them:

> If you have masters among you who can answer for the virtue of your children, I should be very far from advocating you sending them to a monastery; on the contrary, I should insist upon their remaining where they are. But if no one can give such a guarantee, you ought not to send children to schools where they will learn vice before they will learn science and where acquiring learning of relatively small value they will lose what is far more precious—their integrity of soul. . . . Are we then to give up literature? you will exclaim. I do not say that; but I do say that we must not kill souls. . . . In fact, the choice lies between two alternatives: a liberal education which you may get by sending your children to the public schools, or the salvation of their souls which you secure by sending them to the monks. Which is to gain the day, science or the soul? If you can unite both advantages, do so by all means; but if not, choose the more precious.[16]

In addition to the monastic schools, and in some cases even before their establishment, there were a few parish schools. Theodoret talks about the school founded by the priest Protogenis (4th Century), where writing and shorthand were taught, besides religion. Protogenis used the Psalter and the "teaching" of the Apostles for reading material and not mythological texts.[17] We also have records about another Protogenis, a priest of Edessa (c. 150 A.D.), who taught the children of his parish elementary Christian subjects, writing, reading and singing.[18] Schools like the ones described above were few in number and were usually the result of a few industrious priests' effort. Later the local synod of Carthage (419) ordered parish-priests to establish schools, teaching the children reading.[19] The same legislation is repeated by other local councils and much later by the Ecumenical Synod of Constantinople (861). The repetition of the same legislation probably indicates that it was not satisfactorily carried out.

But, as mentioned previously, the Monastic and Parish schools were not many. The use of secular schools was "a necessary evil," and there were always some who protested their use. Nevertheless even Basil, the son of a bishop, had attended a secular school and before him Athanasius of Alexandria was sent to such a school by his protector, Alexander the Bishop of Alexandria. This was the solution given to the first problem of the above mentioned dilemma.

II. The second problem, concerning Christian teachers, was also rather complicated. There was not a single and generally accepted answer to it. Time brought changes in the Church's attitude towards it. At first, the teaching profession was listed among those other professions which catechumens had to give up before they could be baptized. Tertullian justifies this approach. St. Hippolytus of Rome tended to be more flexible, in cases where the catechumen had no other trade by which to live.[20] Probably, Hippolytus reflects the general position of the Church, which was quite lenient. It is known that Origen was a grammar teacher, and that Anatolius (3rd Century), who became Bishop of Laodicea, held the chair of Aristotelian philosophy in Alexandria. The presbyter Malchion also was the head of a school in Antioch and at the time of Julian the Apostate (362), Christians held chairs of philosophy in both Athens and Rome. This shows how relaxed the Church was in allowing Christians to be teachers.

Finally, it is worth noting that the Church of Syria and the Churches of other "barbaric lands" as opposed to the Greek Church, undertook the task of developing their own national literature, educational system and, in general, national culture. Bishop Rabboula, (d. 435), established a Syrian school in Edessa,[21] which was not a catechetical school. Frumentius (4th-5th Century), raised Ethiopian to the level of a written language. Mesrob, according to tradition, did the same for Armenian and Georgian, Qurdutsat of Arran probably for Hunnish, and Ulfilas for Germanic. The Church as an educational institution needed its members to be literate to some degree in order to accomplish its purpose. When they were not, the Church undertook the task of making them literate. Thus, Christianity passed the classical culture to the average citizen. This was something Julian the Apostate had failed to realize.

C. Christian Education

To the early Christians, the term "a Christian education" meant the acquisition of a deep knowledge, which went beyond the intellectual, the emotional and the scientific. It was an "experienced knowledge" of the "revealed truth," as it was expressed by the Bible and the dogmas of the Church. At the same time, Christian education also meant a moral training according to Christian Laws. The idea of Christian education can first be found in St. Paul's Letters: "Ye fathers, provoke not your children to wrath: but bring them up in the nurture and admoniton of the Lord." [22] The term "Christian education," was first used by Clement of Rome (A.D. 96) in his letter to the Corinthians: "Your children should partake in Christian education." [23] Ignatius also suggested that it was the parents' duty to give their children education and instruction.[24] To this call, Monica, the mother of Augustine, Nona, the mother of Gregory of Nazianzus, Anthusa, the mother of three bishops (Basil, Gregory, Peter), and four saints, together with so many other parents responded eagerly. Libanius the Rhetor wrote about them with admiration: "Ye Gods of Greece, how wonderful are the women of the Christians." [25]

I. The Family's Role

Basil believed that preliminary education should be provided by one's parents during the first years of childhood, and he underlined the importance of the mother's role. Chrysostom added that if the child learned good moral habits when he was very young, his later moral education would not be so laborious. He went further and outlined the proper methods for a good Christian education, making use of examples, admonition, commands,[26] etc. Chrysostom also suggested that a good way of receiving a Christian education was to read from the Bible and to sing the Psalms, which would have had a good effect upon the child's soul. Singing psalms was also recommended by Eusebius of Caesarea[27] (263-340), and before him by Justin the Martyr. In his educational treatise *The Right Way for Parents to Bring Up their Children*, Chrysostom suggested the telling of biblical stories to children as a powerful means of education and he even proposed a way for telling these stories. Thus, the parents' teaching on the one hand their example of a virtuous Christian life on the other, provided the basis for a Christian education which the Church was to complete.

II. The Church's Role

a) Catechumenal Schools

The early Church faced the problem that the majority of those who wanted to become her members came from pagan families and therefore lacked even an elementary Christian education and knowledge of the new faith. To remedy this, the Church undertook the task of educating them before their baptism. The systematic instruction, which was a preparatory stage for baptism was called "catechism." During catechism one learned the simple elements of the Christian faith and morals and later in the fourth century, one was also given an elucidation of the more profound Christian mysteries, as is made clear in the 4th Prebaptismal Catechesis of Cyril of Jerusalem. The candidate had to be introduced by one of the faithful, called "anadochos," and be examined by the "doctors" who were in charge of the catechumens, to ensure that clear spiritual motives led him to enter the Church. The "anadochos" was responsible for the candidate and played a very important role during the process of his catechesis and even after the candidate had been baptized. The course of catechism took two or three years for adults[28] and four years for the children of baptized Christians and catechumens. People who had newly expressed their desire to join the Church were instructed privately, in the basic elements of the Christian faith. Those who had already been admitted as "hearers" were allowed to attend a part of the Liturgy which contained: i) Readings from the Law, the prophets and the Psalms. ii) Lessons from the Acts or Epistles, the Gospels and a homily by the bishop.

After his sermon the bishop would bless the catechumens and the deacon would say: "Go out, ye catechumens in peace," and then the Liturgy would continue. The instruction of catechumens, as well as of the faithful was connected with worship so closely that it is very difficult to separate them. Those who were ready for baptism received a special pre-baptismal instruction, including the Lord's Prayer, the Creed, the doctrines of the Holy Trinity, Incarnation and the Psalmody.[29] The teachers tested them by asking questions. In addition, the catechumens were required to train themselves in moral practices and ascetic life.

The instruction of catechism took place several times a week in the portico of the Church. The teachers were known as "catechists," and and they were clergymen or laymen like Tertullian. These schools were called catechumenal schools and they were found wherever there were Christians from the very beginning of Christianity. They were open to any serious applicant of any social class, of either sex and of any age.

However, religious training did not end with baptism. It continued throughout life, delving deeper and deeper into the meaning of Christian life.

b) Catechetical Schools

Besides the "catechumenal schools" the Church also had what were called "catechetical schools." These were institutions providing both theological and classical education on an advanced level.

i) The School of Alexandria. The most celebrated among the educational institutions of Christian antiquity was the school of Alexandria. It seems to have been in existence from quite an early date. In the middle of the second century it became an important school of scientific theology. Pantaenus (180 A.D.), Clement of Alexandria, Origen and Didymus the Blind were among the more illustrious names associated with it. Origen was the one who glorified it, but Clement was the one who paved the way for him. Origen divided the school into two parts, one part being for catechism, which he put under Heraclas,[30] and the other for more advanced studies in which he taught higher theology, exegesis, philosophy, geometry, and arithmetic. Certain other subjects, such as grammar, rhetoric, music and astronomy were also taught in the school of Alexandria.[31] The students used the library of the University of Alexandria, known as the "Museum." This school of Alexandria, which was called the "Didascaleion," owed its success not only to the outstanding scholars who taught in it, but also to the atmosphere of the entire city, which was essentially intellectual. Men in it lived only for letters.[32] Finally, the school of Alexandria was something more than the "Didascaleion." It represented an intellectual and theological movement which appeared and reached its zenith in Alexandria and which followed Origen to Caesarea. The "Didascaleion" of Alexandria was for the most part an offshoot of the school of Alexandria.

ii) The School of Antioch. This was the second most important school. It was founded by Lucian the Martyr (240-312), and it gave to the Church the outstanding exegetes Diodore of Tarsus, Chrysostom, Epiphanius, Cyril of Jerusalem and the heresiarch Arius. Antioch was also a center of Greek learning which offered to the Antiochian theologians excellent facilities for the study of philosophy and rhetoric. In comparing the two schools, the Alexandrian one was more Platonic with some elements of Stoicism whereas the Antiochian was more Aristotelian. The first was more idealistic with a philosophy of dreams and mystery while the second was more realistic, with a philosophy of logic and system. The one used the allegoric interpretation of the Scriptures, while the other had a critical and literal interpretation.

iii) The Schools of Nisibis and Edessa. The school of Edessa was the most important of the non-Greek catechetical schools. According to tradition, St. Ephraem the Syrian was its founder, when he transferred his school from Nisibis to Edessa, which was within the Byzantine Empire. He did this when the city of Nisibis fell to the Persians in 363 A.D. The school of Nisibis became Nestorian in its theology, since many Nestorians, having found protection under the Persians, gathered there.

The general character of the whole school of Edessa was monastic. Even its buildings were organized as a monastery.[33] The curriculum contained biblical studies, historical studies, exegesis, Greek philosophy and rhetoric.

Besides the above mentioned catechetical schools, there were many others, such as the school of Caesarea, founded by Origen, the school of Seleucia, the school of Rome. Some of these were seminaries for clergy, but they were not as important as the schools of Alexandria and Antioch. The Church itself could be called a school of very great importance. Christianity intended to reform the whole world and it chose teaching as one of its primary methods of accomplishing this. The living relationship of bishops, priests and monks was an everyday instruction of no less importance. In this sense, every zealous clergyman and monk was an important school. From the background of such a Church, with so many activities, problems and conflicts, monasticism arose. To accomplish its own purposes, monasticism had to form its own educational system. In some respects it was similar to the one used by the early Church, but in many other respects it was different. This system will be critically examined in the following chapters.

Chapter II

Theoretical Ideas on the Main Questions of Education of the Early Fathers

None of the Early Fathers ever wrote a treatise specifically on theoretical questions pertaining to Education. Their ideas regarding education are scattered throughout the vast Christian literature. Therefore, it is necessary to search for, systematize and analyze these ideas that are found in the early works of the Fathers in order to produce a complete picture of their theoretical system of education.

For this purpose the following divisions will be used, so that the material may be more clearly and profitably dealt with:

A. HEREDITY AND ENVIRONMENT
B. DIVINE GRACE
C. THE POSSIBILITY OF EDUCATION
D. THE PURPOSE OF MONASTIC EDUCATION
E. ASCETIC LIFE AS A MEANS FOR MONASTIC EDUCATION

A. Heredity and Environment

By "heredity" is meant the continuity from generation to generation of certain elements of germinal organization. However, this term is unknown to the Fathers. Instead, they use the word "physis," meaning "nature" to indicate what is meant by the term "heredity."

The second term, "environment," is a very broad one and is by no means easy to define. In this study it is used to indicate all that lies outside the individual; that is to say, other persons as individuals, society with its structure and institutions, plants and animals, any and all objects in general, geographical climate, etc. This term is not used by the Fathers in its broad meaning. Instead, they used other terms which refer to parts of that larger whole such as "training," "directing," "education," "social intercourse," etc. They refer more often to the social environment than to the physical one.

The Church Fathers were quite aware that heredity and environment were two factors which played a very important part in the personal development of each individual. According to them, man inherits imperfections as well as aptitudes. St. John Climacus, the famous master of souls and director of consciences, stated this view very clearly in his *Ladder*:

> . . . some, I know not why, . . . are by nature, I might say, prone to temperance or silence or purity or modesty or meekness or contrition. But others, although almost their own nature itself resists them in this, to the best of their power, force themselves . . .[1]

The above passage is quite surprising since it states the view that man inherits aptitudes, an idea which is seldom found in the works of the Fathers. The Patristic Literature, fighting against sin, emphasizes the negative side of heredity, affirming that we inherit imperfections, which are regarded as the result of "original sin," or Adam's sin," i.e., the disobedience and the sinful choice of the first man, Adam, who ate of the forbidden fruit. Thus, by this disobedience Adam was deprived of his communion with God and became corrupted. This corruption is passed down from generation to generation and it pervades the entire human nature, soul and body. Abba Macarius says that this exists in all human beings[2] and pushes them on towards sin. This forms the "other law," the "law of sin" which is in our members, as St. Paul wrote, and which wars against the "law of mind." [3] For this reason, men "are ready and disposed to join in evil" [4] rather than in good. The degree of this evil tendency differs from person to person and its nature is not so much compelling as it is impelling. This thought is expressed by St. Macarius the Egyptian, who says in one of his Homilies: Our nature is capable of receiving good and evil. The power of evil is hortative and not coercive.[5]

Further, the Patristic Literature makes clear that "passions," as it terms the imperfections and, in general, the tendency towards sin, are not our primordial nature.[6] Man is free to succumb to, or to react against it, a fact which makes him responsible for his actions.[7] The monk's life was nothing more than a continuous effort to overcome this evil tendency. The monastic education, on the one hand, aimed at systematizing this effort and, on the other, at developing the good traits which are also inherited from one's ancestors. Some of these good traits were intelligence and "virtues." [8] St. Basil wrote: "Virtues exist in us also by nature and the soul has affinity with them not by education but by nature herself." [9]

The term "by nature" here is synonymous with that of "by birth." At an earlier period Abba Paphnutius (4th Century), stated explicitly that some people have intellectual inclinations, while other people have moral inclinations.[10] The "virtues" do not exist in a developed stage, but as a seed, as "proneness" and "fitness" which is made clear from the previous fragment and from Clement's of Alexandria writings: ". . . above all they ought to know that, by nature we are inclined toward virtue, not that we possess it by birth, but that we are suitable for acquiring it." [11] The degree of progress depends upon the training one receives and upon his personal effort. In his *Letter*, St. Macarius, wrote: Divine Grace has arranged things in such a way that everyone participates in spiritual progress according to his own opinion, his own will, his own labor and effort.[12]

The inherited aptitudes, imperfections and other characteristics are what differentiate one person from another and make each person unique. This uniqueness is taken into account even by the Canon Law, in order to determine at what age a child becomes responsible for his actions. Thus, Timotheos, in his *Canonical Answers* says that a child is responsible for his actions once he has reached a certain maturity, usually around age 10 or 11 or so. A later canonist, Balsamon (1105-1195), explaining why Timotheos did not set a particular age, said that it depended on the nature of the child.[13]

A number of passages in the ascetic texts indicate that the Desert Fathers regarded "environment" as an important influencing factor in a person's development. St. John Climacus notes with amazement that social intercourse, which is a part of one's environment, is so powerful that it affects and sweeps away one's natural disposition very quickly. It is possible that for didactic reasons the author of the *Ladder* overemphasized the molding power of environment, and was not expressing the general viewpoint on this matter. Although the Fathers do not say to what extent environment influences one's development, it appears that they did not regard it as an all-powerful factor. Even St. John Climacus at another place in the *Ladder* accepts that heredity forms the framework on which environment attaches itself and molds the character.[14] However, the Fathers thought that a good environment could be very helpful for a person, and that a bad one could be detrimental. In the *Apophthegmata* it is written: "the one who goes to a perfumery, even if he buys nothing, partakes in the pleasant odour."[15] Therefore the Desert Fathers took steps to create a beneficial environment in their monasteries, and they encouraged earnest relationships between novices and senior monks, the latter being the monk's "perfumery." Monks were to strive for such an intercourse and to avoid by all means any interchange with "false brethren."[16] This environment also was produced by the whole general structure of monastic life.

B. Divine Grace

The Fathers viewed human development as being three-dimensional. Two of them, heredity and environment have been discussed. The third dimension is Divine Grace. In Christian theology the term Divine Grace means the free and unmerited favour of God as manifested in the salvation of sinners, and the bestowing of blessings. Divine Grace works mainly upon those who are organically connected with the Church and who try to live according to her teaching. But Divine Grace also works outside the Church upon men who often ignore it, and who do nothing to obtain it. The present subsection deals mainly with the "grace" which is called in Latin "gratia praeveniens," however the so-called "gratia sanctificans" or "sanctifying grace" will also be briefly dwelt upon.

Meritoriously speaking, the Fathers regarded Divine Grace to be the most important among the factors which have an influence upon a person's development. Furthermore, Divine Grace, besides having a direct influence upon man, also managed or controlled the other two influencing factors. Thus the Fathers considered many things to be the result of Divine Grace, which a modern scholar would consider to be the result of the other two factors. A very early monastic document explicitly asserts the primacy of Divine Grace. This is the *Vita Prima* of St. Pachomius. In it can be found the words of his Disciples spoken with admiration and astonishment:

> We used to think that all the saints were so many

> by God from their Mother's womb, holy and unalterable, and not of their own free will and that sinners could not live godly, because that was how they were created. But now we see the goodness of God clearly in the case of this our Father that from pagan parents, he is become so God-fearing, and is clad in all the commandments of God . . . Let us die and live with this man, for he guides us rightly unto God.[17]

The very same passage is also quoted in the *Apophthegmata.* The Church sings in its hymnology "whenever God wishes, the natural order is defeated" and this is the supernatural law that the Fathers of the Church witnessed every day.[18] All in all, in patristic thought, every step towards kindness was a gift from above. According to the Fathers, Divine Grace was the force which guided the good hereditary and environmental character antecedents and enabled educational efforts to succeed. Christ's words: ". . . without me you can do nothing," [19] were always in their minds.

To summarize, one can say that the Desert Fathers regarded a person's development to be the result of three factors: Heredity, Environment and Divine Grace. St. Macarius wrote:

> It is not only by the divine power and Grace, without man's collaboration and effort one would make a progress; nor it is only by one's own power, effort and strength, without the collaboration and help of the Holy Spirit, that the perfect will of God and the full measure of all freedom and purity shall be reached.[20]

To what extent each of these influencing factors contributed to one's development is not clear from the patristic texts. However, the Fathers emphasize strongly the role of Divine Grace, placing it above the other two factors.

Comparing now their point of view to the modern one, we find that on the question of the formative influences of heredity and environment their ideas are similar to our own. A well-accepted modern opinion on this question is that:

> A person, any person, and all his physical, mental, and cultural characteristics, is a product of the interaction of nature and nurture, heredity and environment.[21]

Obviously Divine Grace is not accepted by scientists as an influencing factor upon man's development. However, many of the features grouped under the term "grace" by the Fathers are generally regarded by scientists as constituting environmental factors.

C. The Possibility of Education

The recognition on the one hand that a person from birth has some bad as well as good natural dispositions and the acceptance on the other hand that a person's character could be molded by the influence of his environment and contacts with other people, emphasizes the possibility of education and also at the same time its necessity. Early Patristic Literature takes for granted that education had a great influence on a person's character. Clement of Alexandria, in a moment of enthusiasm, said that proper education leads to heaven, and the *Apophthegmata* state that a good word has the power to make even an evil person good and an evil word able to make a good person evil.[22] Further, the Desert Fathers believed that education applies to the body as well as to the soul and that it has a strong influence upon the whole life. Macarius the Egyptian insists that by a proper training we can make ourselves virtuous, and John Climacus says that with a good training we can limit even our natural needs, such as food, sleep, etc.[23] But the Fathers warn that the task of education is very difficult, that it takes time and should be done patiently, gradually and with leniency.[24]

Further, the Desert Fathers, dealing with the question of age, express their opinion that the results of education are more satisfactory when education takes place during the childhood years. Whatever has been impressed on the soul at that early period, when the soul is easily molded, tender and obedient, like wax, is hard to efface later. Thus a person's education should be started at an early age, when, as Basil says, the nature of a child is very tractable.[25] St. John Climacus reiterates the same point and remarks that the education which has been received as a child has a definite influence, either positive or negative, upon his development in the monastic life. Finally, in his treatise *On Vainglory and the Right Way for Parents to Bring Up their Children*, Chrysostom dealing with the same question also explains why the early years are most important, saying that at that age the "soul is delicate," and when good instruction has been impressed on such a soul nobody is able to efface it, because it is as hard to efface as a seal. In like manner, a novice's first years were very essential for his further development. Thus, the first period of initiation into the monastic profession was regarded as a very crucial stage and for this reason much attention had to be paid to it, both by the Elder and the Disciple.

The Desert Fathers, recognized, however, that education was not able to solve every problem. Its power was limited,[27] and it is not clear from the patristic texts to what extent this was so. Thus, some people, although having received a good moral education all their lives are not yet "good" persons.

D. The Purpose of Monastic Education

It is essential to make a clear distinction between the purpose of monastic education and the purpose of monasticism. The former can be better understood if one understands the latter.

Monasticism in general has the same purpose as Christianity; that is to form Christian characters in people so that they may be ready to enter the Kingdom of Heaven. Thus, the Christian life was understood as a participation in the divine life. Monasticism, however, had its own means for obtaining the above goal. Moreover, although the Desert Fathers may have expressed their aims in different ways, in the final analysis the aims of both monasticism and Christianity in general can be seen to be identical.

For the early hermits, for instance, the avowed purpose of their profession was to recover Adam's condition before the fall,[28] since man's fallen condition was regarded as an "unnatural" condition. In the *Life of St. Antony* it is written that Antony persuaded the animals not to disturb his peace or ravage his garden. Here we have before us the picture of a relationship between Antony and the animals, which marks the recovery of Adam's condition before the fall. It is written about Antony that "he was in complete equilibrium as is one who is governed by reason and who also abides in his natural condition."[29] Other Fathers preferred to say that the purpose of monasticism was to reach the state of "hesychia," meaning "quiet" or "tranquillity," or the state of "apatheia," meaning "mastery over one's passions."[30] If a monk reach the state of "apatheia," he could consecrate himself to "theoria," meaning "contemplation," of which the continuous "intellectual" prayer is the highest expression. Others said that the purpose of monastic life was for the monk to obtain the "gifts of the Holy Ghost"; an opinion which is repeated by St. Seraphim of Sarov, the late Russian mystic of the 19th Century. Besides this, the Desert Fathers also believed that it was the aim of monastic education to help the novice to reach his goals as quickly as possible. Therefore they applied all the proper means they had at their disposal to help the Disciples in their difficult task.

In a later chapter, the several methods they used will be looked at more closely, however, for the present, the most important means, which was called "ascesis," will be dealth with from a theoretical point of view.

E. Ascetic Life as a Means for Monastic Education

The term "ascetical life" means an austere way of life, involving: restraint in eating, vigils, silence, absence of comfort, obedience, discipline, etc. The basis for this ascetical life can be found in both the Old and the New Testaments.[31] In the writings of the Apostolic Fathers, however, the elements of ascetical life appear according to the following order:

I. The determination of certain days of fasting.
II. The determination of fixed hours for prayers.[32]
III. The avoidance of marriage, especially of a second marriage,[33] and
IV. The renunciation of the "world," i.e., the material world.[34]

In the early monastic sources the monastic life is frequently identified with "ascesis," which means "exercise," "practice," "training," etc. However, in monastic texts it is used as a technical term, to indicate the hermitical and monastic life and its practices.[35] The monks were called "ascetics," meaning those who have left the "world" and are practicing continence, partaking an austere life.[36] This word was normally used in Greek literature to denote "one who trains or practises an art." The monk, according to St. John Climacus' definition

> . . . is he who within his earthly and soiled body toils towards the rank and state of the incorporeal beings. A monk is he who strictly controls his nature and unceasingly watches over his senses . . . A monk is a mourning soul that both asleep and awake is unceasingly occupied with the remembrance of death.[37]

This definition echoes clearly the ideas of the very early hermits as they were expressed by Abba Zacharia, who said that, in his opinion, a monk is the one who "forces" himself in everything.[38] Therefore it can be seen that asceticism had an intimate and essential involvement in monastic life.

The bodily toils were the price paid for the gifts of the Holy Ghost. The *Apophthegmata* declare therefore: "give blood and receive spirit." [39] Further, these toils were the "tools of virtues," or more correctly they were a means to the goal of monasticism, since they purified the heart and mind, attracting Divine Grace.[40] But ascetic life was never an end in itself. Ascesis was simply the contribution of the body to the struggle of the soul in trying to reach its goal, as Isidorus of Pelusium interprets it in one of his letters. Since some monks often made ascesis an end in itself, the Ascetic Literature insistently warned them that its value was only relative.[41] For example Abba Theodorus once said to a certain brother, who in an assembly boasted of his severe fasting, that it were "far better for you to eat flesh in your cell than to make such a boast among the brethren."

Monastic Literature makes a clear distinction between the divine ascesis and the demoniacal one. The former is distinguished by its moderation, while the latter is a thoughtless and excessive ascesis which leads not to purification of the heart but to a demoniac egoism. The golden rule of monasticism was for monks to avoid extremes.[42] Ascesis had to be accompanied by discretion, which Nilus called the "source, root and head of every virtue," and which Sophronius of Jerusalem (ob. c. 638) called the "queen of all virtues." The purpose of ascesis was to kill the passions and not the body. As Abba Poemen once said to Abba Isaac: "We have been taught to be not body killers, but passion killers." [43] This statement is somewhat reminiscent of an answer given by the monk Dorotheus, who, when asked by a visitor why he was destroying his body, answered: "It kills me, I kill it." [44] Such extremes were not rare in early monasticism, especially in Syria and Mesopotamia, where asceticism took bizzare forms. The great advantage of the ascetic life was that it allowed the monk to participate in an uninterrupted communication with God. This resulted in a continuous and unbroken devotion to prayer.

Moreover, the monastic mind, as opposed to that of the Gnostic and Manichean, never considered matter itself to be evil, since God was regarded as the Creator of all matter. Greek dualism never became a belief of the Orthodox Christianity. Nothing is bad; God would not have created evil.[45] Therefore one should not avoid nor cast away possessions simply because they are evil in themselves, but one should dispense of them properly, since they could be the instruments for sin. Moreover, monks did not exclude the possibility of salvation outside the monastic ascesis. They often were informed by angels that although they had been living an ascetical life for a good number of years in the desert, they had not yet reached the spiritual state of some laymen living in the world.[46] Ascesis was a negative physical education, which aimed at weakening and purifying the body corrupted by sin and preparing it for the resurrection. The monks believed that "... as the body is weakened, so much the soul flourishes." Varsanuphius asks: "... for what is fasting but a chastening for the body to enslave the healthy body and make it weak on account of the passions?"[47] However, Basil was one who, on the other hand, warned that the monk should maintain his body in a healthy condition, otherwise, the soul would not be able to look at the divine.

Although none of the Desert Fathers ever wrote a treatise on education *per se*, they seem to have been quite aware of certain concepts of education, about which they had their own thoughts and ideas. These thoughts and ideas, perhaps originating in part in Old Testament and Greek philosophy, were in many respects similar to our own. However, they introduced one new factor in the development of a person's character, that of Divine Grace.

Chapter III

Elder and Disciple

The two main and important monastic ranks dominating both early and later monasticism are those of the "Elder" and the "Disciple." They appear as hierarchical ranks in the earliest monastic literature. Monastic tradition determined that all the Elders should pass from the Disciple stage to that of the Elder. This transition was to be of long duration. The positions of Elder and of Disciple were descripted by a number of Greek terms, each of which seems to reflect the outlook of the period on those two ranks. For example, the term "geron" and "pater," are used of the Elder of a very early period. The first of these occurred many times in the *Apophthegmata* and in Evagrius' writings. The term "geron," meaning "an old man," is used to express not so much the age of the Elder, as the prudence of his maturity. At the same time, the other term "pater," meaning "father," was used to indicate the Elder's paternal love and his interest for his Disciple who was his spiritual son. Besides these the terms "hegoumenos" and "abbas" were also in use. The latter is a Syriac word of a Semitic root meaning "father" and it is used in monasticism with the meaning of "spiritual father" even in the 330's, as is evidenced by its frequent occurrence (in its Coptic form) in the Meletean Correspondence.[1] The term "abbas" occurs in many early monastic sources and is still in use, as are all the above mentioned terms.[2] The other term "hegoumenos" meaning "to be at head of," is a technical monastic term meaning "abbot." It came into use when monasticism passed from its eremitical state to its cenobitical one. In his Rule, Pachomius states that nobody is to walk in front of the "hegoumenos."[3] The same term also is used by Nilus the Ascetic, John Moschus, John Climacus, and many others. The term "hegoumenos" was applied only to the head of a monastic community, whereas the term "geron" applied to any hermit who had under his instruction one or more Disciples, or to monks who were venerable because of their virtue and asceticism. The "abbas" was a title given only to those distinguished monks who through their life and teaching had become teachers and professors of the whole of monasticism. It is noteworhty that in the first chapters of *Vita Prima Pachomii* the term "abbas" is not used of Pachomius, since he was considered to be too young.

Finally, there were two other terms, which were used in reference to the head of the community.[4] One of them is the term "archimandrite," meaning the "head of a fold," as monasteries were called in Syria and Mesopotamia. This indicates that the term had been introduced probably from Syria. The term occurs twice in *Historia Lausiaca*, in Basil's writings, in Epiphanius' *Panarion* and in other early texts. Sometimes an Archimandrite was the head of a group of Monasteries. This was especially so in Palestine.[5] The second one was the term "proestos," meaning "to be at the head of," and became a technical monastic term meaning the leader of a monastery.[6]

For the Disciple the term "archarios," was used which means "beginner" or "novice." Later when Cenobia came into existence, and the virtue of obedience was regarded as the most important and necessary virtue of the monk, especially for the novice, the term "hypotaktikos," meaning the "one who obeys," came into use, indicating that the Disciples' first task was to obey his Elder. Finally, the term "mathetes" meaning the "one who is learning" or "Disciple" was also commonly used.[8] The usual Latin terms for the Elder were "Abbas," "Senior," "Maior," and "Pater," and for the Disciple, "Discipulus" or "Novicius." [9] The Coptic monastic terms for "Elder" were "hello," meaning "an old man," and "nog," meaning "great"; for "abbas" the term "apa" was used. Syriac terminology is also interesting. The Syriac term for "hegumenus" was "meshablana," meaning "leader," or "resh daira," meaning the "head of the monastery," i.e., "archimandrite." The novice was called "talmida," meaning the "one who is learning" and monks in general were called "dairara," meaning "dweller." This chapter will look first at the position of the Elder in monasticism, his significance, his role and his qualifications, and then at the Disciple, his identity, the motives for his withdrawal into the desert, his need for an Elder and finally his individuality.

A. Elder (Teacher)

The Significance and the Role of the Elder

Even the first pioneers of monasticism like Antony, Pachomius, Arsenius, etc., felt the need for a guide and a spiritual adviser, because they realized that the life of a hermit was a very difficult one and it was almost impossible to become learned in it without the guidance of a Master. The Monastic tradition and literature emphasized very strongly the necessity of having an Elder. In one of the *Homilies*, attributed to St. Macarius the Egyptian (4th century) it is stated that the students of the Kingdom of Heaven always need a guide,[10] otherwise they labour in vain. A Monastic proverb, recorded by Palladius, warns: "Those who are not under the law of the governors shall fall like leaves." St. Cassian (5th Century) also, who voices the ideas of the Egyptian Desert, says that it is foolishness for someone to think that it is not necessary to have a teacher for the spiritual profession, since for every worldly profession we need one. The allegorical St. John Climacus in his *Ladder* writes with fervour:

> Those of us who wish to go out of Egypt and to fly from Pharaoh certainly need some Moses as a mediator with God and from God, who standing between action and contemplation, will raise hands of prayer for us to God. So that guided by Him we may cross the sea of sin and rout the Amalek of the Passions. That is why those who have surrendered themselves to God, deceive themselves if they suppose that they have no need of a director.

Not only novices but also experienced monks, were expected to obediently follow the advice of Elders, and not to become lawgivers for themselves. The Elder, who was looked upon as God's instrument, was regarded as the only means by which one could reach the state of "hesychia" (quietness), which is a very advanced stage of spiritual life. The Disciples by trusting in him were thought to be able to find peace by following his regulations.[12] An Elder could not be replaced by books, since his task was not simply to lecture but to know and analyze the inmost thoughts and acts of his Disciples and finally to regulate their life in the way that seemed best to him. It is readily discernible why such an important task was both very difficult and full of responsibility. As Gregory of Nazz. notes, this task was more difficult than simply learning how to submit yourself to rule.[13] St. Nilus, explaining the reason for this, remarks that the difficulty arises from the "variety of human habits" and the "cunning of our thoughts." Varsanuphius (6th Century) in one of his letters addressed to his Disciple John characterizes the Elder's task as a real "head ache."

His Election

During the early period of anachoritism a monk could only gain the title and the authority of an Elder on the basis of his progress in spiritual life. In the early cenobia, however, when the Abbots came to the point of death they usually suggested or appointed their successors, as it is clear from the *Life of Pachomius*, and Cassian's *Institutions.*[14] At a later time, the Abbot, whose position was equal to that of the Elder, was elected by the senior brethren of the Community and by the Elders of other Monasteries, as St. Basil the legislator of Estern Monasticism commands in his Rule. The Abbot was the "spiritual Father" of the community; however, he was responsible not only for spiritual but also for material problems such as finance, organization, and administration. He was a kind of monarch in his community and was elected for life.[14] A second-in-command also was elected in order to replace the Abbot, when he was absent or sick. If the Abbot ever erred, the senior brethren of the community were to admonish him. Any minor mistake of his did not give the brothers the right to replace the Abbot. Only if he fell into heresy did they have this duty, by virtue of the seventh canon of the Synod of Ephesus (431) which commanded that bishops and clergy must be removed from their positions if they embraced a different faith.[15] This was also stipulated by the 17th Canon of Nikeforos of Constantinople, (806 A.D.)

His Qualifications

Since an Elder's inexperience could utterly destroy his Disciples, ascetical literature gives a detailed description of what the Elder should be. The foremost requirement was that he should be full of love for his Disciples, to the extent that he would be ready and willing to be burnt and poured as a libation for them.[16] and also he should be eager to work very hard, as a "merciful Father" and good guardian for the benefit of his Disciples, who were to be regarded as the "Despot's children" i.e., God's children. At the same time he was to be very well versed in theory and in practice, in whatever concerned spiritual things.[17] For this reason an Elder had to have actual experience and practice in his job, the prerequisites for any tutor. Merely knowing the habits of ascetical life, i.e., how and when to pray, the diet, etc., was certainly not sufficient for someone to become an Elder. It was required of him constantly to exercise his mind and to study by himself, investigating the truth of his speculations and he was not to undertake any educational responsibility before he thought himself fit to solve the problems regarding ascetic life.[18] Ignorance is unforgiveable for a Tutor. "The one who does not know and has made mistakes which should be punished will be punished, because he has not learnt."[19] Consequently, the Elder had to have long experience in the desert and know the secrets of desert life as well as to have, by reason of his holiness, charismatic gifts which would enable him to direct the novices or even the experienced monks, who had not yet attained the perfection of monastic life, in their problems and difficulties. In order for a monk to have the above qualifications to be able to undertake the task of teaching and leading others, he should be an old man and have spent some decades in the ascetic life. In the *Life* of St. Pachomius there is an episode which shows the early monastic attitude toward the teacher's age. Once when all the brothers of St. Pachomius' Monastery had come together, as was their practice, to listen to his lecture, Pachomius asked a certain brother by the name of Theodorus, who later became his successor, to speak to the brothers. However, some of the older brothers hearing this, decided to leave, saying to themselves: "Because he is a novice and teaches us, we will not listen to him."[20] But the same text tells us that Theodorus had been living in the monastery for twenty years, and yet they still regarded him as a "novice" after twenty years of monastic life! The above elements constitute what was required of the Elder's background and characteristics. He had to be gentle, patient, and tolerant of others' faults. It was not fitting for an Elder to be angry, since such a "Shepherd disturbs and destroys rational souls." [21] Varsanuphios asks: "If thou hast me as a Father and teacher, why also as wrathful? For a father is compassionate, not having wrath at all, and a teacher is long-suffering and a stranger to wrath." [22] Further the Elder had to be clement and not examine every minor incident, since otherwise he would not be God's imitator. Besides this, an Elder was to be a living picture of every virtue, as St. Nilus the Ascetic wants him to be. He should teach by his virtuous life and not by his words. In particular he should be a model of extreme humility to them and never be egotistical or sarcastic.[23] Rebukes must never spring from a secret desire to dominate the Disciples for his own egoistic ends, but from his concern for them. His autocratic powers should not make him a despotic person. "The Superior must not be exalted by his high post, lest he fail to get the blessing which is promised to the humble, or by his pride, fall into the condemnation of the devil." [24] A good example of such a humble Abbot was St. Pachomius. He used to say: "Just as a dead person does not say to other dead people—I am your leader,—likewise I never regarded myself as being the Father of the brothers, but [that] only God Himself was [their father]." [25] The Desert Fathers, having in mind, on the one hand, the above mentioned difficulties of the educational task and the required qualifications and personal characteristics and the fact that the Elder was liable to give account before God for every one of his Disciples, on the other, often strongly refused to undertake the role of an Elder. They did not consider themselves able and worthy enough to accomplish such an important and heavy task. Very representative of this is the answer which was given by a certain monk when he was asked to undertake the Abbot's office: "Forgive me fathers that I may mourn for my sins; because I am not a suitable person to take care of souls. This task is for the great Fathers like the Abba Antony and the others." [26] Varsanuphios also wrote: "I do not want to become anyone's Abbot or anyone's teacher. Forgive me brothers and pray for me." [27] Only "the perfect" were supposed to be Elders and teachers of "Juniors," and no one considered himself a perfect monk. Very characteristic of this way of thinking is the example of some Abbots who secretly left their monastery and went to another without saying who they were and asked to be accepted as novice monks. The reason for doing this was not only their strong desire to live in humility but also the responsibility which they felt they had before God for every one of their Disciples. Basil, echoing the belief of fourth century Monasticism in this regard, writes in one of his Rules:

> He who is entrusted with the charge of all must remember that he is to give an account of each. For if one of the brethren falls into sin, and is not told of God's judgment by the Superior, or if he persists in his error, and is not instructed in the way of amendment by him, his blood will be required of him.[28]

The Elder's struggle was twofold: To save his own soul as well as the souls of his Disciples.

Finally, it is worth mentioning that the Desert Fathers were called "teachers," and "educators," as evidenced by the occurrence of these terms in the *Apophthegmata* and in St. Alexander's *Life.* The latter states that Alexander "became educator and teacher to every one." [29] All of these references prove that these men were conscious of themselves as educators and that their contemporaries recognized them as educators. Their educational theories and how they applied them to actual practice, are dealt with in another chapter.

B. Disciple (Student)

Who He Was and Why He Fled

The persons who withdrew from the cities and went to the desert were zealous Christians who came from every social level. They were men and women of all ages and of all levels of education. Looking for the motives of their withdrawal one finds that a strong desire to meet God had led their steps to the desert. One of the early hermits, Macedonius, expressed in a very epigrammatical way, the reason for his flight when he was asked by a huntsman what he was doing in such a barren spot. He said: "I too am a huntsman . . . I am hunting for my God, and yearn to capture and enjoy Him. Him I desire to see and never will I rest from this my gallant huntings."[30] His withdrawal was also a reaction against the growing secularization of the Church, as it was mentioned in the introduction of the present study. The Greek hermits or those who had a Greek outlook on life expressed the reason for their flight in a more intellectual way saying that they were trying to reach the state of "Theoria," meaning "contemplation," as Evagrius Ponticus explains in his treatise on prayer and other works. The same term "theoria" is used also in the *Apophthegmata* in the story of Abba Arsenius:

> When Abba Arsenius was in the palace, he prayed to God and said, 'O Lord direct me how to live,' and a voice came to him, saying, 'Arsenius, flee from men and thou shall live,' and when Arsenius was living the ascetical life in the monastery, he prayed to God the same prayer, and again he heard a voice saying to him, 'Arsenius, flee, keep silence and lead a life of silent contemplation.' "[31]

The term "theoria" or in Latin "contemplation," occurs in the writings of the Cappadocian brothers, Basil, and Gregory as well as in the writings of Peter Damascene (fl 775), and later in the writings of Gregory of Sinai

(13th Century), but it is not very prominent in the *Apophthegmata.* The *Apophthegmata* deal more with Egyptian and Coptic monks, who certainly did not have as much education as the Greeks did. They used another term "hesychia," meaning "tranquillity," which was a simpler concept and which presupposed perfect devotion to God, and finally a renunciation and withdrawal from the world. Besides the world, in order to reach the state of tranquillity, the monk was to renounce himself and become a so-called "dead person," i.e., a person without any worldly desires. In the *Apophthegmata* there is a story about a monk who was asked to give a few words of advice to some people. He answered: "I do not have anything to say, for I have died (and) a dead person does not speak."[32] When another monk was asked to go to his village and inherit his father's property because his father was dying, he said, "Myself, I have died for the world before him; a dead person does not inherit from a living one."[33] The term "hesychia" is used by Origen, by Basil, and his brother Gregory, by Chrysostom, by Nilus the Ascetic and by many of their successors. The life of a hermit who lived in "hesychia" was called "hesychios bios" and the hermit was called "hesychast" or "solitary one," as we find in Palladius' *Life of St. Chrysostom*, in Nilus and John Climacus' writings and in many other places.[34]

In regard to the actual words which they used to express their withdrawal from the world, we find that they used various terms. The most common ones were "flee" and "flight." These denote the flight which they made to save themselves from the dangers of the world. In *St. Antony's Life* the phrase "coming out of my own" is used,[35] and it is repeated by Ephraem the Syrian. St. Athanasius also uses the word "apotassein" meaning "to renounce," which occurs in St. Basil's *Letters*, Chrysostom's writings, and Palladius' *Laus. History.* Similarly the word "aparneisthai," is also used, meaning "to deny something," and it is always accompanied by the word 'world' or 'myself.' Finally, the most common term used by ascetical authors is the term "anachorein" and "anachoresis," meaning "to withdraw" or "flee" and "withdrawal" or "flight" respectively. The term occurs in *St. Antony's Life* in the works of Eusebius of Caesarea (died 340) entitled "*Demonstratio Evangelica*," in Isidorus of Pelusium's *Letters*, in the *Apophthegmata*, in Palladius' *Life of St. Chrysostom*, in St. Nilus' *Letters*, and in many other early sources. The sociable Basil uses this term and explains that "anachoresis" does not involve only a geographical change of position but more completely a change in one's entire way of life.[36]

The early monks, as it has been said above, were called "hesychasts" because they practised "hesychia." But at the same time they were called "anchorites," because they withdrew from the world. This term occurs as early as the time of Justin the Martyr (martyred in 165), and later in *St. Antony's Life*, in the *Apophthegmata*, in Palladius' *Laus. History*, and in the writings of Evagrius and Nilus. In Latin the term is "anachoreta."

The Search for an Elder

The postulant's privilege and duty was to knock at the door of a holy man and seek counsel. St. Basil, the great monastic legislator, set this duty upon all who enter upon the monastic life, that they should search for an Elder and attach themselves to him:

> "Seek out," he says, "with much care and thought a man who will be a safe guide to thee in thy manner of life, who knows well how to lead such as are journeying towards God, who is rich in virtues . . . and being wise in the Holy Scriptures." [37]

Long journeys on foot, either alone or with company, were undertaken in order to find a well-known "Father" to whom they usually said: "we have hastened to come to you because we have found in your words so many things that never even entered our minds."[38] They put themselves under the Elder's command with great confidence that this spiritual Father had the "words of life" and loved men.

Great care had to be taken in choosing the spiritual Father, in order to choose the proper one, who would be able to help the monk overcome his faults. "Let us judge the nature of our passions and our obedience . . . and choose our spiritual Father accordingly," writes St. John Climacus.[39] An experimental period was permissible before the choice. After that, he had no right to judge the manner in any way at all, even though he may see in him some slight failings. If the Elder's orders were not clearly against the Word of God, the novice had to obey him, even to death.[40] Moreover, they were not allowed to change the Elder once they had chosen one, but they were supposed to keep the same one forever: "A monk whom Jesus Christ has united to his superior, by the bonds of faith and love will preserve this union even at the price of his blood," wrote St. John Climacus, although at another place he is more flexible.[41]

However, the novice monk could also be refused by the Elder as one of his Disciples. Ascetic literature is full of such examples. Characteristic is the story about St. Paul the Simple, who remained without eating for 4 days outside the cell of St. Antony, being refused as St. Antony's Disciple. Similar to this is the story of St. Pachomius, when he knocked at the door of the hermit Abba Palemon, the old man cried out rudely: "Why are you knocking?" The youth Pachomius said, "Father, I desire you to let me be a monk with you." The old man did not welcome the aspirant with open arms, but instead launched a discouraging account of the solitary vocation. "You cannot be a monk, for it is no small thing to embrace the monastic life,"[42] and Palemon went on to say that many others who came for the same purpose were not able to stand it and went back shamefully when he described briefly the purpose and the way of the monastic vocation:

> Scripture orders us to pray and fast in order that we may be saved. The Rule of Monasticism, as we have been taught by our Predecessors, is as follows: at all times we spend half the night and often from evening to morning—in vigils, reciting the words of God, and doing much manual work, with thread, hair or palm-fibre, so as not to be importuned by sleep and to provide for our bodily need; whatever remains over and above what we need, we give to the poor . . . Now that I have taught you the law of monasticism, go and examine yourself on all these points. See if you are capable of doing what I have said.[43]

St. John of Damascus (9th Century) faced the same difficulties, when he decided to exchange the minister's office for the monastic cell.

This denial did not spring from the Elder's unwillingness to help the novice but, as has been said in the previous sub-chapter, it sprang from the Desert Fathers' consciousness that the Elder's task was very difficult and from their sincere conviction that they were unable to undertake such a responsible task, on the one hand, and from their belief, on the other hand, that it was not a small thing to embrace the monastic life. This denial was at the same time a test of the postulant's desire to become a monk. If it was a simple and temporary enthusiasm, it would vanish before the first difficulties, and at the same time, these difficulties strengthened the desire of those who really wanted to become monks. From this point of view, it was an excellent preparation for the monastic profession.

In the works of Cassian we read that "the postulant must first be outside the door for ten days" and that "they each call the postulant 'him who is renouncing this world.'" The next step was to examine whether he had abandoned all his property and his family. After that, they taught him the rules of the monastery and exchanged his clothes for the monastic dress which consisted of a robe and a girdle.[44] Then the novice was put under the charge of an Elder and was not allowed to mix with the monks. He had to look after the visitors in the guesthouse for a year, although one would expect to hear that the novice did not have any relation with the layman. They did it, perhaps to test further the postulant's decision to become monk. This custom still continues in the monasteries of Mount Athos.

In his shorter Rules, St. Basil prescribes that all members of the monastic community were to decide whether the postulant should be admitted or refused, and be present at the reception of the novice monk. The Superior did not have the power to receive him without the knowledge of the brethren. Admission to full membership in the brotherhood took time, since the procedure was gradual. The novice had to undergo a period of probation in order to become familiar with the monastic life and its meaning as well as to give his Superiors a chance to observe the novice. St. Pachomius' Rule Determines that the period of probation must be three years, a period which also is demanded by the 5th Canon of the Synod of Constantinople (A.D. 861). If the applicant was a child, Basil required that the "chiefs of the Church" should be among the witnesses of his reception. The presupposition for a child's reception was that he had reached the age of discretion. Early hermits wanted the postulant to be mature and not beardless. They were not favorable to the idea of accepting children to the monastic profession. They regarded it as an omen of decline and for this reason they used to say the following proverb: "When you see children in scete, take your cloaks and leave." [45]

Once the novice had chosen his spiritual father, in the case of an independent hermit, or was put under a senior monk by the abbot, in the case of a cenobite, he was asked by the monastic tradition to consider him as an almost sacramental person and to obey him "not because of his seniority or wisdom or virtue, but as the symbol of our Lord Himself."[46] Disciples were aware that their Elder loved his brethren "as a nurse cherisheth her own children." For this reason the novice would open his heart to his Elder, and put himself in his hands like pliable material in the hands of an artist. The *Apophthegmata* warns the Disciples not to misuse their Elder's love and lose their respect or obedience for him. Abba Isidorus said that the novice should love his teacher like a parent and fear him like the government.

But if there is any word which expresses most characteristically the Disciple's relationship with his Elder, it is the word "obedience." Obedience was one of the three monastic ideals and according to St. John Climacus, it was among the first things which the novice monk had to learn after renouncing the world. The ideal of obedience was advanced in depth, not in Egypt[47] but in Asia Minor, by St. Basil, who set great store by it. A definition of obedience given by St. John Climacus is as follows:

> Obedience is absolute renunciation of our own life, clearly expressed in our bodily actions. Or, conversely, obedience is the mortification of the limbs while the mind rests alive. Obedience is unquestioning movement, voluntary death, simple life, carefree danger, spontaneous defence by God, fearlessness of death, a safe voyage, a sleeper's progress. Obedience is the tomb of the will and the resurrection of humility . . . Obedience is an abandonment of discernment in a wealth of discernment."[48]

To the ascetic mind obedience did not exclude freedom. Obedience led to the purification of mind and heart, which is the true freedom. As Clement Alex. defines it: "Freedom is to control our passions." Their obedience was not blind, passive nor unreasoning, but it was a trusting obedience that their Elder was an interpreter of God's will and knew the true path to peace and purity of mind and heart, which was true freedom for them.

A very characteristic example of obedience is the one found in Cassian's *Institutions:*

> "We hear of a certain John the Short, who, when bidden by his Superior to water a log of firewood, spent a whole year at his task, carrying water from a distance of two miles, as though it had been a divine command." [50]

Cassian lets Abba John give a biblical explanation of obedience, saying:

> "I mean that I should take no thought of the morrow, and submitting myself completely to the Abbot, seem in some degree to emulate him of whom it is said: 'He humbled himself and became obedient unto death,'(Phil. 2:8) and so be able humbly to make use of his words: 'For I came not to do my own will, but the will of the Father who sent me' " [54] (John 6:38).

A theological interpretation of obedience which was developed later considered that just as Adam had fallen because of his disobedience to God's commandment, we should follow the opposite path, one of obedience in order to reach Adam's state before his fall, which as we have seen is the purpose of monasticism.[52]

In some cases the postulant was required to make a written application for admission to the monastic brotherhood, in which he had to declare that he would walk in obedience. This is clear from one Coptic manuscript which reads:

> In the name of the Father and the Son and the Holy Ghost, I, John and Shenoute, my brother, (I) write unto my father Apa Zacharias and our father Apa Jacob and Apa Theodore and all the brethren according to their names, (saying,) since I myself have desired in my heart's desire, together with my brother, not by constraint, but by my own decision, and . . . have requested our father Apa Zacharia and Apa Jacob, that their pity might reach me and my brother, so that we might be worthy to take part in prayer with them, but they desired to require a declaration at our hands, namely,

that we will walk in the ordinance, after the manner of all the brethren that walk in obedience (and) that we will go nowhere without asking (leave), nor will (do) aught whereat your heart should be pained beyond (contrary to) all the brethren. If I shall commit a fault and do aught whereat your heart should be pained, ye it is that command and (may) cast me forth. And further, I will not let any . . . in unto me, whereat your heart should be pained. I, Theodore, this humblest one, I am witness to everything written therein . . . I, John, the humblest one, who have already written this declaration with my own hand, I assent thereunto according as it is written." [53]

The Disciple's Individuality

After what has been said about the self-denial, the obedience and the austere way of life of the monk, one may think that the individuality of the novice would disappear completely. Such a thought, however, is unfounded as we will see. The Desert Fathers, never forgot that "Man is a most varied being with many customs" as Gregory of Naz. has said. As educators, they tried to apply what is called today "the individualized method of teaching." [54] In the *Apophthegmata* is reflected "their great respect for the variety of personal vocations and ways. They did not seek to impose hard and fast rules upon the novices reducing all to an arbitrary uniformity." [55] They appreciated the different "ways" and "diversity of gifts" which the "one and self-same Spirit, worketh, dividing to every man severally as He will.[56]. This variety of souls is acknowledged by Clement,[57] John Climacus and indeed most of the Fathers. Isidorus of Pelusium (5th Century) for example, said: "All people are not happy with the same things, neither are all cured by the same medicines." [58]

The postulant's personality and his spiritual development were taken into account and he was helped by his Elder to choose the way of life best suited to him. St.

John Climacus, living at the end of the "Desert Period," gives us a picture of the mature, contemplative, introverted and eremitical outlook of early monasticism. He writes in his *Ladder*:

> Those who have really determined to serve Christ with the help of spiritual Fathers and their own self-knowledge, will strive before all else to choose a place, and a way of life, and are habitation, and exercises suitable for them. For community life is not for all, on account of greed, and not for all are places of solitude, on account of anger.[59]

Among the other factors which were taken into account when a novice was accepted, was his age. In the *Ladder* we read that the monks should not all live in the same place but in different places, according to their age. The same work also gives the information that St. Antony prescribed various diets for his Disciples according to their condition.[60] Pachomius had divided his Disciples according to their character, as we read in his Rule:

> They each shall consist of 24 associations and each of the associations thou shalt call according to the Greek letters, from Alpha and Beta and Gamma and Delta in their order, and the gentle ones call I and the perverse call X and thus according to their order and their kind and their arrangement and the life of each association in its character, call them by name.[61]

Besides their age, physical needs, character, development, etc., sex also was taken into account as is clear from Gennadius' writings where he says: "He (Evagrius) composed also a doctrine of common life, suited to cenobites and synodites and to the virgin consecrated to God, a little book suitable to her religion and sex." A more careful study of the past shows that many of the "modern ideas" are similar to those of Classical and Christian Antiquity. It is obvious that in early monasticism there was a clear distinction between the Elders and the Disciples. Ascetic literature emphasizes the significance of the Elder's role, determines his qualifications and his duty. A number of terms attributed to the Elder indicate that his role was mainly educational. At the same time other terms attributed to the novice indicate that his life was to be a continual learning. The Disciple was free to choose his own Elder, but he had to remain with him and obey him in all matters. In the school of the desert the individuality of every novice was taken into account.

Chapter IV

Teaching Methods and Discipline in Monastic Education

A. Teaching Methods

A careful study of the monastic educational acts, as they are evidenced in the *Apophthegmata*, and in the monastic literature in general, shows that the Desert Fathers took serious account of the "individuality" of the novice. In doing this, they did not use just one or even a few methods, but a rich variety, applying different methods, according to the age, spiritual state, and character of the novice. In general, they took into account the entire personality of the one to whom they were addressing themselves. The kind of monastic life which the novice had entered, i.e., anchorite, cenobite, etc., also affected the method of teaching. In the prologue of the book of *Varsanuphius and John* (6th century), the following passage is written:

> But when we are intending to read the things in this book, we ought to know that some of them were spoken to anchorites, and some to those in Cenobia, and others to those in choir, and others again to priests and Christ-loving lay folk; and some to younger men or novices, some to the already advanced in age and exercised in the habit, and others to men approaching the perfection of virtue, as each was suited to hear. For the same teachings do not suit all alike . . . Often also they answered

> having regard to the infirmity of the thought of the questioner, coming down oeconomically to his level, so that he should not fall into despairs . . . [1]

The prologue goes on to say that we must not receive as a general rule "the things thus said by way of 'condescension' to particular people."

Two centuries earlier another celebrated father who devoted his life to monastic practices, St. Gregory of Nazianzus (330-390), writing in a style reminiscent of a modern educator, said that different souls must be treated with varying instruction and guidance. Some are led by doctrine, others by example. Some need the spur and others the curb. There are some who benefit from praise and others who benefit from blame. But both must be applied in season, otherwise, if they are out of season or unreasonable they are injurious. "Yet," Gregory said, "there are others who need encouragement and still others who need rebuke, in public or in private according to the person." And Gregory went on to say that sometimes we should keep a close watch, even on the minutest details and at other times we should not take notice, but while seeing, appear not to see, and while hearing, not to hear. In some cases we must even be angry, without feeling anger, according to the nature of the individual being guided. Finally, others are best helped by a teacher who acts humbly, treating his students on a proper level and aiding them to conceive readily a hope for better things.[2]

Gregory's ideas, however, can also be found in earlier patristic writings, as for instance in Clement's *Instructor*, where Clement says that the tutor of humanity, i.e. Christ, uses every means possible, i.e. admonition, reprimand, rebuke, reproval, threat, healing, promise, forgiveness, etc.[3]

One of the monastic authors, St. John Climacus, also repeats the above points, advising his namesake, the Abbot of Raithu, to be discreet and neither to tell all of his Disciples that the road of a monk's life is narrow and broken, nor to tell all of them that the yoke is easy, but to examine them and speak to each of his Disciples accordingly.[4]

The educational task, according to the Desert Fathers, was not an easy routine which could be applied in the same manner to all Disciples, but it was a laborious process, involving many methods, which were to be applied in various manners, according to the nature of the Disciples. This does credit to the Desert Fathers who, living in a period when little attention was paid to the individual, emphasized by words and actions, the necessity of individualized education. The variety of teaching methods, and the organization used by the monks were two of the most important characteristics of the monastic educational system.

This sub-chapter will deal with the most common and important teaching methods, which will be discussed according to the following outline:

- I. Instruction by Verbal Means
  - a) General Methods
    - i) Lecture
    - ii) Dialogue
    - iii) Admontion
    - iv) Counselling
  - b) Specific Methods of Preserving Ideas
    - i) Parable
    - ii) Allegory and Symbolism
    - iii) Apophthegms
- II. Instruction by Non-Verbal Means
  - a) Symbolism of the Monastic Habit
  - b) Silent Methods
  - c) Observation of Nature and the Empirical Method
  - d) Personal Example
- III. A test of the Monastic Educational System
  - a) Self-examination
  - b) Confession

I. Instruction by Verbal (Oral or Written) Means

The importance and necessity of verbal instruction is very obvious, since it forms the foundation on which every action in our life, and the whole of life itself, should be based. In the New Testament the need for verbal instruction is emphasized, and certain of the Church Fathers regarded it as the first step towards salvation. Because of this, they constantly devoted themselves towards the effort of instruction, which had as its result the creation of a vast Patristic Literature. The Desert Fathers, in particular, believed strongly in the power of "logos," (word, speech). In the *Apophthegmata*, the request "Tell me a word," which both novices and Elders alike addressed to famous masters of the desert, is a very common request.[6]

According to the patristic texts, two basic principles must preside during instruction. The first is the principle of gradual progress and the second the principle of individual instruction. The first principle was emphasized by St. Basil who remarked that instruction and education in general should follow a gradual process starting from elementary and easy lessons to more advanced ones.[7] This thought was echoed by Isidorus of Pelusium,[8] a contemporary of Basil, and by John Climacus, two centuries later.[9] The second principle was emphasized by Basil's brother, Gregory of Nyssa, and Basil's close friend Gregory of Nazianzus. In his *Magna Catechetica*, composed about 385 A.D., the former underlines the necessity of instruction and at the same time notes that the same method does not suit all people.[10] The other Gregory is more detailed on this point and he writes that men and women, young and old, rich and poor, rulers and ruled, wise and ignorant, the wrathful and the meek, the successful and the failures, the cowardly and the courageous do not need the same instruction and encouragement.[11] Hence the Desert Fathers used many means of instruction. The most important ones were lecture, dialogue, admontion and counselling.

a) General Methods

i) *Lecture*. Although lecturing was very common in

the early Church, it was not common in the first stage of monasticism (anchoritism), at least in a formal way. However, it entered monasticism with the establishment of cenobitism, probably because the great number of the brothers of a cenobium required a method proper for collective teaching. Pachomius, the "Father of Cenobitism," commanded that within each monastery three weekly lectures were to be given by "stewards";[12] one on Saturdays and two on Sundays and two other lectures by the housemasters, on Wednesdays and Fridays. These lectures were something similar to the catechisms of the early Church. The brethren gathered round the master, listened to him explaining the Scriptures, and then each of them went back to his cell in silence to meditate on what he had heard and to learn it by heart.[13] These lectures had a general character and they referred to many different matters. As regards their style, the Fathers tried to be as simple as possible, in order to be understood by everybody. Oral lectures were supplemented by written ones taken from various books, and letters were also exchanged when oral instruction was impossible. St. John's *Ladder* is a letter to his namesake, the Abbot of Raithu, who asked him to write something for the benefit of his monks. Another good example is the book *Varsanuphius and John* which is a selection of Varsanuphius' letters to John. Finally, the two thousand letters of Isidorus of Pelusium, which are regarded as products of a cultured spirit and a burning heart, and the thousand-odd letters of Nilus of Ancyra (d. 430), are examples which show that the monks recognized written as well as oral instruction.

ii) *Dialogue.* The dialogue was another method used by the Desert Fathers. It took place between the Elder and one of his Disciples. It was generally concerned with specific questions or personal problems which the asking monk placed before the Elder. In Pachomius' *Life*, it is clear that prior to retiring for the evening there was a time for conversation which was confined to the subject of the instruction received during that day. In the *Apophthegmata* also, the dialogue method is found. Many times, the Fathers, instead of giving dogmatic answers to the questions from their Disciples, started conversation with them and following the method of Socrates, through other questions, made them give answer to their own questions.[14] Thus, when a military man once asked Abba Mios if there was repentance for a sinner, the Abba said to him: "Tell me, when your cloak is torn, do you throw it away?" The man answered, "No, I sew it and I use it." Then the Abba said to him: "Therefore, if you spare your cloth, will not God spare his own creation?"[15] Dialogue was a simple and effective method which the Greeks had used long before the Church Fathers. It makes the pupil conscious of his own ignorance, and leads him towards a deeper truth, which has not been presented to him ready-made, but drawn out of his own mind. The pupil would hold that truth very firmly, since he himself, with the help of his teacher, has discovered it.

iii) *Admonition.* The early ascetics were not very eager to admonish or to reprove the wrongdoing of brothers, unless they asked their advice. This we see when Serapion paternally with patience admonished one brother who was in trouble.[16]

The Cenobites, however, had a different point of view on this matter. They felt that they were responsible for their brothers and therefore should admonish them when necessary. Basil laid a great deal of responsibility on any Elder who did not admonish and reprove erring brothers.[17] This is one more point which differentiated anchoritism from cenobitism.

iv) *Counselling.* This method also was not applied by the early anchorites to the same degree as it was applied by cenobites. Personal guidance presupposed a close relationship between the Counsellor and the Disciple, which did not exist to a great degree among the early hermits. The bond between Elder and novice was almost voluntary.[18] What did exist, was more on the level of admonition than on the level of personal guidance. Personal guidance, as the monks understood it, was something much more than admonition. It was the responsible obligation which the Elder undertook in walking together with his Disciple along the "steep and broken path" towards perfection. This guidance took place mainly during confession, which besides being a spiritual "medicine," was also a counselling session.

St. Basil was the Father who lifted personal guidance to the level of a science. In his Rule he declares that the task of education and guidance needs knowledge and experience, more than anything else. In his ascetic works recommending the principle of individual guidance, he remarks that, because of the peculiarity which every human being has and because of the infinite number of human types, it is impossible for someone to fix one method of instruction for all people.[19] Basil points out that instructors cannot treat all their Disciples in the same way, and, as K. Mouratides says, he recommends the use of several curative methods, which must be chosen according to the bodily and psychic strength of the Disciple being guided.[20]

b) Specific Methods of Preserving Ideas

When the Desert Fathers were lecturing, admonishing or counselling, besides expressing their thoughts directly, they used many other means in order to be better understood and more effective in teaching their Disciples. The most important means were the use of parable, allegory and symbolism, and apophthegms.

i) *Parable.* A parable is a developed simile in which one thing is likened or compared to another thing of a different kind for illustrative purposes. In a parable, the words "like" or "as" are often used. The Desert Fathers used parable very often in order that their ideas be more easily understood, and to avoid the theoretical teaching which was more laborious and whose results were sometimes doubtful, especially if the listeners were illiterate, as a good number of the early monks were.

In Pachomius' *Life*, it is written that this saint used parable very often, and one example of them is given.[21] In the *Apophthegmata* also the use of parables is very common. Thus Abba Poemen in order to teach the efficacy of the divine Logos, used this parable:

> The nature of water is soft, the nature of stone is hard, but drops of water can bore through a stone. In the same manner, the Word of God is soft, and our hearts hard, but the heart of him who listens to the Word of God very often opens up and fears God.[22]

ii) *Allegory and Symbolism.* Besides the parable, the ascetic fathers also used allegory, which is a kind of developed metaphor which conveys a deeper meaning than the surface one presents by means of symbolism. Alexandrians, and particularly, Origen, as well as Antiochians, very often used allegory as a method of exegesis, in contrast to literal interpretation.

For ascetics, the use of allegory was a moot point. St. Basil, for instance, objected to the use of allegorical interpretations. He wrote:

> I know the laws of allegory, though not from my own works but from the works of others. Some preachers do not concede the simple sense of Scriptures. They do not call water water, but something else. They interpret a plant or a fish as their fantasy wishes. They change the nature of the reptiles and wild beasts to fit their allegories.[23]

But in spite of what he wrote, he himself sometimes uses allegory when it suits him. Among the ascetics, Isidorus of Pelusium also rejected the use of allegory, but again, he also uses it at times.[24] Of the other fathers, Chrysostom and his friend Theodore of Mopsuestia (died 428), rejected allegorical interpretation. The latter wrote a five-volume book *Against the Allegorists* which is lost. In it, Theodore opposed Origen who had systematized the allegoric method.[25] The historian Eustathius (died 337?), also rejected Origen's entire allegorical exegesis. The reason for this strong opposition to allegory was the fact that an enigmatic allegorism could lead the brothers to wrong conclusions.

Nevertheless, allegoric interpretation of biblical events occurs very often in the *Apophthegmata.* Abba Kronios, for instance, interpreted allegorically the meeting of Elisha and the Shunamite, as well as the story of the burning bush. This kind of interpretation can be found frequently in St. John's *Ladder.* A good example of this is the following:

> You will not be delivered from Pharaoh and you will not see the heavenly passover, unless you continually eat bitter herbs and unleavened bread. And bitter herbs—this is the coercion and pain of fasting; and unleavened bread—this is a mind that is not puffed up.[26]

In Patristic writings, besides the allegorical interpretation of Scriptures, there can also be found an allegorical reference to nature.[27]

A teaching method somewhat similar to allegory was that in which symbols were used by the Fathers in order to make a point. In a letter written by Ammonas, a Disciple of Antony, one can read that novices received new names as a symbol that "the old man of sin" was now dead and that the novice was a "new man of grace." [28] Another example was the custom of cutting novices' hair, called tonsure, which was aimed at teaching the novice that he should cut off all secular thoughts.[29]

As time passed, many acts of adoration and items which were used by the monks acquired a symbolic meaning. This tendency, however, was not confined to the monks. The rest of the Church as well began to give symbolic meanings to many things, as for instance, to the compounding of Chrism.[30]

iii) *Apophthegms.* Finally, the Desert Fathers, besides the other methods, used to express their ideas by repeating apophthegms or sayings of famous monks. These were the answers of famous Masters given to questions of novices, senior monks or even laymen. In the apophthegms, the Master intended to give a short "rule," expressed in a few words, in order to meet the individual need of the inquirer. For this reason, the sayings of the Desert Fathers should not be considered as hard and fast rules which apply to all persons in every situation, but as general statements about monastic life and as broad general principles.

About the end of the fifth century, an anthology of such sayings of the most famous Masters of the Egyptian desert was compiled. It was probably in the sixth century that this compilation was arranged in alphabetical order according to the names of the persons whose works and words were recorded in it. The purpose of this anthology, entitled *Apophthegmata* or *Gerontikon*, was educational, as is stated clearly in its introduction.

II. Instruction by Non-Verbal Means

When the novice had received enough instruction by verbal means and was able to understand and value the meaning and the merit of actions, the Desert Fathers started to teach him by actions as well. This sub-chapter deals with four such teaching methods.

a) Symbolism of the Monastic Habit

The most important day for a monk was the day he received the monastic habit. The habit, being interpreted symbolically, became one of the most important non-verbal means of teaching. The special garb of the monks appeared very early in the history of monastic life, being evidenced as early as the beginning of the fourth century. Pachomius, for example, was said to have been clothed at once in the monastic habit by Palamon, as soon as he was accepted.[31] The Melitian monks used the sleeveless tunic already in the 330's, as is clear from the Melitian Papyri.[32] The 16th Canon of the Pachomian Rule also determined that the novice, after having been taught the Psalms and "the knowledge the (other) brothers (knew)," was to be dressed in the monastic habit. The Pachomian habit consisted of a sleeveless linen tunic, held together by a cincture, a sheepskin cloak, a small cape to which was connected a hood, a belt and sandals.[33] In the *Apophthegmata*, the term "schema," meaning habit and in general monastic life, occurs many times, as it does also in Evagrius' and Serapion's (ob. 362) writings as well. The monastic habit is often called "angelic habit" and "heavenly dress."

Besides a detailed description, Cassian also gives a symbolic interpretation of each item of the monastic habit. For instance, he says that the child's hood was to remind the monk of his obligation to live as a child, and the sleeveless tunic meant that the monk must cut away earthly desire.[34] In Sozomen's *History* (written 439), another symbolic interpretation of the Pachomian monastic habit can be found.[35] One century later in his *Doctrina I*, Abba Dorotheus (6th Century), gives a more advanced interpretation of the monastic habit, from which it is clear that at that time it was a more detailed garb than the Pachomian one.[36] From the same period we have another description and interpretation of the monastic habit, by Maximus the Confessor (580-662), who gives the additional information that black had already been accepted as the proper color for monastic garb.[37]

The monk, wearing the monastic habit, and having in mind the meaning of each item, always had with him an indefatigable teacher which reminded him of his obligations and the way in which he was supposed to live at every moment. Abba Dorotheus wrote to his fellow monks: "Let us live and act according to our (monastic) habits in order not to wear an alien habit." [38] (In the previous chapter he had already remarked that the monks should know the meaning of each item.) Thus, when the monk was putting on his belt, he was reminded by it that he should be ready at any time to serve the will of God.[39] The black colour of his habit reminded him that he is a person mourning for his sins and that he must be unknown to the "world." In the same manner every item reminded and taught the monk of something important regarding the way of monastic life.

In his *Longer Rule*, question 22, St. Basil gives also a general discription of what he thinks the Christian dress should look like and points out three useful functions of it:

a) It is a way of confession of the Christian profession.

b) It serves as a way of communication among Christians, who should recognize each other by the simplicity of their dress.

c) It makes all Christians, especially the weak ones, very careful about their lives, since their dress announces their faith and society expects them to live according to the Christian moral standards.

b) *Silent Methods.* Sometimes the Desert Father's proceeded to silent, puzzling, even incomprehensible actions in order to impress their Disciples and attract their attention. When the interest of the brothers was roused to a peak, they would explain the meaning of their actions. The ascetic literature has preserved many of these enigmatic actions, which were an unusual way of teaching. In the *Apophthegmata*, the following story is found:

> Once a general assembly was held in the scete for judging a brother who had committed a fault. Though the rest of the brothers were accusing the monk, Abba Peor was listening and saying nothing. Finally, he stood up, took two bags, one small and one large, and filled them with sand. Then he put them over his shoulders having the small bag on this chest and the large one on his back. The fathers did not understand what he was doing and asked him to explain. His answer was: "The bag with more sand is my faults which I put behind me, because I want to avoid laboring and morning for them, and behold I have

> put the small faults of my brother in front of me and I am prating and criticizing them. But I should not act like that. I should care for my own sins and supplicate God to forgive me." Then all the brothers stood up and said: "Truly this is the way of salvation." [40]

Again:

> Another hermit, Abba Anour, lapidated and then praised a statue in order to teach his fellow monks that they should be invincible (unassailable) by both insult and praise like the statue.[41]

In the *Apophthegmata* there are many other similar examples.

In their teaching, the Desert Fathers always tried to be very expressive and supervisory in order to be better understood by their people. The Desert Fathers believed so strongly in the educational power of example that they thought that even God uses the method of example, through his angels, in order to teach his chosen people. God, for instance, wanting to show a monk how useless moral actions are when their motives are not pure, led him to a place where the monk saw a man who was drawing up water from a well, which he was pouring out into a cistern. But this cistern was connected to the well and the man was laboring in vain to fill up the cistern. In the same manner, the text says, the ones who do many moral actions but do not have clear motives, are laboring in vain, since they will not have any heavenly reward.[42]

c) Observation of Nature and the Empirical Method

These two last methods are mainly self-teaching methods, which the novices were taught to follow, since nature and experience were regarded by the Desert Fathers as two good teachers. When Antony was mocked by a philosopher because he could not read, Antony answered him, saying: "My book, o philosopher, is the nature of created things, and it is present when I wish to read the words of God." [43] From that early period, monks saw nature and the whole universe as a powerful educational tool, which at the same time illustrates the dignity of the Maker and the divine Providence. In his *Hexaemeron*, Basil urged man to observe the animals,[44] for, as Cyril of Jerusalem wrote, the bees and the other animals are always giving emblematical lessons to man.[45] This kind of observation enabled monks to study carefully their environment and to employ in their teaching successful natural images with meaning for men, as is found in the *Letters* of Ammonas.[46] He was regarded as the most instructive and precious source for the history of the earliest Monasticism in the Desert of Scete. But it should be pointed out that at the same time, many monks, turning their attention inwards, overlooked their physical environment. In the *Apophthegmata*, Amma Sarra is said to have lived above a river for sixty years and never to have taken a side glance at it.[47] Such things occurred even more often among the hesychasts.

Greek philosophy had seen the physical universe as a "theophany" and its reverence towards nature was great. For the Christians the beauty and the order of the visible world is just a testimony to God's creation and providential care of it. Their emphasis, however, lies on the incarnation of God as a man, and on his Church. Thus, the ecclesiastical cosmos and not the natural cosmos has the main importance in the Christian understanding of reality. It is for this reason that we can speak of Christianity as an anthropocentric religion.

Finally, life itself was a convincing teacher.[48] The mistakes of the monks, the "war of Satan," and the actions of the Holy Ghost, taught them many things. St. John Climacus writes that:

> Those who have been humbled by their passions may take courage. For even if they fall into every pit and are trapped in all the snares and suffer all maladies, yet after their restoration to health, they become physicians, . . . lamps and pilots for all, they teach us the habits of every disease and from their own personal experience they are able to prevent their neighbours from falling.[49]

d) Personal Example

Personal example was the best of the non-verbal methods used in the monastic educational system, and in general one of the most important, since it gave credibility to all the other methods, both verbal and non-verbal. In a way it was the seal upon all that was taught. The early ascetic literature quite often emphasizes the significance which personal example, as a teaching method, had. In Pachomius' *Life*, for instance, Pachomius is said to have led his Disciples by example rather than by precept and by his example to have won their devotion. Abba Apollo also, as Palladius writes, urged some people to lead a contemplative life, and others, to lead a more practical life, showing first by his own actions, what he wanted to teach them.[50] In the *Apophthegmata* can also be found a number of sayings emphasizing the importance of personal example. When, for instance, a brother asked Abba Poemen if he should give precepts to some other monks who were under him, Abba Poemen answered: "... not precepts and commands but let you do the task first. Do not become a lawgiver but a model to them." [51]

The Desert Fathers believed that if someone was not able to profit from their example they would not be able to profit from their teaching either. They regarded personal example as a more powerful teaching method than any verbal one. For this reason they taught what was to be done mainly by example.[52] Abba Sisoes said once to a brother who had asked him to tell him a "word": "Why are you forcing me to speak idly? Look, do whatever you see." [53]

The Desert Fathers as pioneers of "depth psychology," knew that a moral personality had a very strong influence upon one's human environment and for this reason they insisted on the importance of the living and personal example. Abba Poemen once told a brother who asked him what he should do, since his soul did not fear God, that he should attach himself to a God-fearing man, and his presence would teach him to fear God likewise.[54] This idea was repeated by St. Basil who said that a Disciple inherits all the virtues of his virtuous Elder.[55] Basil's brother also expressed this in his writings.[56] Isidorus of Pelusium remarked that a teacher should educate his Disciples by his manners rather than by his words. Personal example was thus thought to urge one towards a virtuous life much more than words.[57] Nilus, the ascetic, was another of the Desert Fathers who underlined the importance of personal example. He noted that personal example and all other actions as well, should be supported and based on a theoretical foundation. Such examples, according to him, had a positive influence even upon stern souls.

Finally, it is worth mentioning that the non-ascetic fathers also regarded personal example as an excellent means of education. Clement of Alexandria, for instance, said that the example of those who have lived a saintly life is the most excellent means of understanding and practicing the commandments.[58] At another point, the same author says that examples are of no small value in determining salvation. He devotes a whole chapter (II, 8) of his *Instructor* in declaring how important examples are in instructing a person properly. Teaching by example was the most highly regarded method of education urged by the early ascetics and the hermits. Modern research has shown that the teacher's personal example has a great influence on the students, who are prone to identifying themselves with their teachers and to imitating them. Therefore, personal contact between the students and the teachers is encouraged by educationists.[59]

Furthermore, the common worship of God should be mentioned here as another educational means. The feelings of repentance, grief, gratitude, excitement and other personal experience produced by the different rituals were of very great value for the spiritual upbringing of the monks. The Church Fathers were aware of the importance of the common worship and they called the liturgical life and practice "mystagogia," i.e., a training and initiation into the mysteries.

Finally, the structure of the monastery and the general monastic climate of the area where the monks were living were powerful means of monastic education. Recent studies, conducted at the college level, have shown that the values, which are part of the social structure of the college are likely to be transmitted to the students, whether it is planned, or not.[60]

In sum, the common worship of God, the monastic program and the structure of monasticism, and in general the life experienced in a monastic community were powerful education means that helped monks to attain their goals in the shortest possible time. The variety of methods did not necessarily make the Elder's task easier, but it certainly made it more responsible. The Elder was expected to be able to choose the proper method and "medicine" for each of his Disciples. For this reason, the Desert Fathers were very demanding, regarding the Elder's qualifications.

III. A Test of the Monastic Educational System

All the previous methods were expected to lead up to: a) self-examination and b) confession. If they did not, there was a fault in the system or the Disciple was unsuitable in some way.

a) Self-examination

One presupposition for an effective confession, and in general for any kind of progress, was for the novice to know himself very well and be able to present himself to his Elder, in order, for the Elder, as a good physician, to choose the right method of instruction and "medicine." This self-knowledge, being "in truth the most difficult of sciences," [61] required a very careful and attentive self-examination. For this reason early monastic literature emphasizes the need for such a careful self-examination.[62]

Self-examination is regarded by Abba Ammonas as one of the first obligations which a monk has and in *St. Antony's Life* it is written: "Let every man daily take an accounting with himself of the day's and the night's doing." [63] And again the father of monasticism said: "Let us each note and write down our actions and impulses of the soul as though we were to report them to each other." [64] Varsanuphius also says that the monk has to examine and watch his thoughts, and he points out how this should be done:

> The searching of the thoughts is in this wise, that when a thought comes, thou give heed to what it gives birth. I tell thee an example. Thou thinkest that someone has insulted thee, and thy thought troubles thee to tell him. Then tell thy thought: "If I tell him, I vex him, and he is grieved against me." So then, I bear it a little, and it passes. But if the thought is not towards a man, but it is in one's self that one thinks the evil, so must one search the thought and say: "The thought of evil leads to hell," and it ceases from thee. And to all thoughts, do likewise. But immediately when the thought enters, search it and cut it short.[65]

So the Desert Fathers did not only emphasize the necessity of self-examination but they also indicated the way to accomplish it as well. Their aim was to fight evil at its very birth. St. John Climacus is also very expressive when he wrote:

> Take up your seat on a high place and watch, if only you know how, and then you will see in what manner, when, whence, how many and what kind of thieves come to enter and steal your clusters of grapes.[66]

The quietness of the desert and the carefree nature of monastic life contributed greatly to a systematic self-examination. Thus, the ascetics, through introspection, discovered and controlled the complicated region of the subconscious, which they regarded as a result of sin. St. Basil, for instance, went so far as to make a distinction between sicknesses which are under the control of the patient's conscience and others which take place in his subconscience. The first step towards recovery from sickness in the subconscious, was for the patient himself to ascertain and accept that he was suffering from such a sickness. The discovery of the sinful depth of the subconscious, with regard to the Last Judgment, led them to an "agony of expectation," which did not bring them to an impasse but rather lifted them up, and made them fight more strenuously against evil.[67]

b) Confession

Monasticism from its very beginning was deeply conscious of sin, as is clear from Antony's words: "This is the great task of man, to take his guilt upon himself in the sight of God and expect to be enticed to the last breath." [68] This consciousness of sin led them to a sincere confession, which was regarded by the early monastic legislators as one of the major tasks of the novices, and later it became a daily practice of the monks.[69]

Besides being an important and necessary sacrament, confession was also the most sacred and significant aspect of the close elder-disciple relationship. For this the task of a confessor was a very difficult but essential one. It demanded a good deal of psychological skill and experience, since, as has been said, it was mainly during confession that personal guidance took place. A good example of such a confessor is Abba Macarius, the spiritual hero of the famous monastic colony of Scete, who once visited a young hermit by the name of Theopemptos, whom he knew to be in trouble. Macarius asked Theopemptos: "How is it with you, brother?" The young monk, afraid to speak the truth, replied in a formalized monastic way: "Due to your prayers it is well." Then the experienced father asked him with a greater urgency: "Are you not being tempted in your thoughts?" "Until now I have been well," was his answer. And the great Abba said in a very pedagogical way: "Myself I have been practicing self-denial for many years and I am honoured by all people. Yet, although I am an old man, the demon of lasciviousness still plagues me." The novice, having been encouraged by this, confessed his temptations: "Believe me, father, it plagues me too!" The old ascetic, pretending that he was plagued by other thoughts as well, moved the young hermit on to confession.[70] Two centuries later, St. John Climacus, expressing the same monastic tactics, wrote in his *Ladder*:

> When someone comes for confession and wavers (to confess his sins), try to appropriate to yourself, with words, but not in reality, his own sin, saying to him: "O brother, do not be sorry, since I myself also have committed those sins." [71]

Confessors very often imposed penalties on those who had fallen into sin. There were many kinds of penalties, for example, some hundreds of prostrations, fasting, extra prayers, abstinence from holy communion for a period, etc. The purpose of these penalties was not to punish the sinner but to help him to understand his fault, on the one hand, and on the other, to give him the chance to prove that he was willing to do something for his sins, as a sign of his repentance. Canon Law canonized the kind and the length of penalties for each sin. But the general practice was to take into account the personality of the sinner rather than what the Canon Law said.[72] St. Basil remarked that confessors must take into account the age of the sinner, his motives, his position, his intention or the disposition of the guilty and his behaviour after his error.[73]

In general, long periods of repentance were rejected by the ascetic mind. When a brother once told Abba Poemen that he had committed "a grave sin" and wanted to repent for three years, the old man replied: "That is too much." Then the brother said: "One year then, surely?" The answer was again: "It is too much." Even forty days was a long period according to that holy man. He said: "I say that if a man repents wholeheartedly and does not repeat his sin, God accepts him in three days." [74] This reply was also given by Abba Sisoes. According to the Desert Fathers, one's disposition was more important than the length of the period of penance. This attitude is illustrated beautifully in the story of Peasia, who had been living prodigally. But when she was visited by the ascetic Abba John Kolovos, she repented and took her way to the desert. However, she died suddenly on the way. The story closes, by saying that:

> . . . the single hour of her repentance was more acceptable than the repentance of those who spend a much longer period in repenting, but who do not show such fervour.[75]

The aim of confession, as the *Apophthegmata* tells us, was to gain peace, by freeing sinners from the burden which weighed upon their conscience. Explaining this in terms of modern psychology, one might say that the monk examining himself carefully and taking confession very often would not push off his sin into his subconscious. Thus, sin did not become an "anarchic" element of his personality. This explains in what way St. Gregory's maxim that confession was an important "medicine" for evil is significant.[76]

Finally, the monk, besides the fact that he would plead his own guilt, sometimes went further and accepted an unfounded accusation, and not rarely would he usurp alien guilt. That is, he would accept the blame for something he did not do. A good illustration of this is the story of Marina, a virgin who, in the dress of a man, was accused of being the father of a foundling. She did not deny the accusation, nor was her innocence discovered until they laid her out for burial.[77] The self-justification, which Adam used, was unknown to the monastic mentality. Rather they were accustomed to self-accusation; a fact which led to their being unaggressive and persons easy to get along with.

The actual term they used for the confessor was "pneumatikos" literally meaning "spiritual man," which term was also applied to senior monks, abbots, and to spiritual counsellors in general. The confessor did not have to be a priest. The belief in short periods of repentance was one more point which differentiated the early ascetics from the rest of the Church as well as from later monasticism.

B. Discipline in the Monastic Educational System

Discipline may be understood either as a system of rules governing conduct or as a training in self-control and obedience to given standards or as an inflicting of ecclesiastical censures and penalties upon the offencer. The term as treated here may pass from one to another of these allied meanings.

Discipline is a very essential element of Christian life, since it basically is a life of discipline and obedience to God's will. The Church Fathers praised its usefulness,[78] and the early ascetics who dwelt together felt its need very early as one can see from the Pachomian Rule. Penalties and rewards were two means by which educators tried to impose discipline upon their students.

I. Penalties

Monastic literature very clearly defines the purpose of penalties as well as the way the use of punishment must be followed. In St. Pachomius' *Life* it is written that Pachomius reproved one of the brothers "for the sake of his salvation." [79]

Thus the penalties were employed for the benefit of the offender rather more than for his revenge, and they also aimed at bringing the other brothers to their senses as John Climacus remarks. Further, Patristic Literature notes that a necessary presupposition for the superior to reprove someone is that he should be in a composed frame of mind, as should the offender.[80] St. Pachomius also adds that the superior has to admonish him first and then proceed to reproach him.[81] In his Rule, Basil gives various degrees of punishment, such as deprivation of blessing, deprivation of food and separation.[82] Furthermore, he remarks that punishments are to be remedial and proportionate to the crime. With the 51st Canon of his long Rule, Basil reflects the thought of the present century quite closely. He writes:

> . . . correction must be applied to the wrong doer after the manner of the physicians who are not angry with the patients but who fight against the disease. Thus, the vice should be attacked and the infirmity of the soul corrected, if necessary, by a more severe regimen. For instance, pride will be corrected by ordering the practice of humility, aimless talk by silence, immoderate sleep by wakefulness in prayer, slothfulness by work, greediness by abstinence from food, discontent by separation from the other brethren.[83]

It is worthy of note that the Basilian system of punishments aimed at replacing a vice with the corresponding virtue. A theoretical basis for these educational tactics is found in the writings of Gregory of Nyssa who wrote that vice does not have its own substance, but it is the absence of a virtue.[84] Consequently, the cultivation of the missing virtue is the best way to fight against the existing malice.

The superior had to take into account who the offender was and then to inflict the penalty accordingly.[85] Thus the Pachomian Rule proposes eighty prostrations for a great habit brother and fifty for a lesser habit brother for the very same offence.[86] St. John Climacus also draws the superior's attention to the offender's personality.

As regards now the kinds of punishment which monasticism employed, there were two main sorts, the corporal and the spiritual. The degree of severity was determined according to the nature of the offence and the personality of the offender, as has been said already. A person, for example, who came to an office late, could not enter the

Church, but he had to lie in penitence on the threshold as the monks came out of the Church. For more serious offences a brother was suspended from public worship. Another category of sins including quarreling or pride, going out without permission, etc., was punished by expulsion. We are told that Pachomius once commanded a monk to take off the monastic habit and leave the monastery.[87] This was a very severe penalty. However, the most severe punishment of any was excommunication by the bishop.

Finally, it should be mentioned that the Fathers very often believed that if we have been punished for wrongdoing here we will not be punished in the after life for our offences. Therefore, abbots were very strict with themselves and with others as well. A good illustration of this is the story of a disobedient Pachomian monk who died and for whom Pachomius did not allow the other brothers to sing the funeral office, nor to bury him with any kind of honour. But he disrobed the dead monk in order to disgrace him, believing that by doing this he was helping the brother's soul to meet a less strict judgment.[88] A careful study of the *Apophthegmata* in regards to punishment, leads one to the conclusion that the early hermits did not permit an erring brother to be disciplined by the others,[89] but this was reserved for his Elder, if he had one. This is a surprising and somewhat impressive behavior which is hard to explain. Perhaps it was because the requirements and the responsibilites of the community were neglected in favor of an individualistic ethic. Furthermore, they thought that the path towards people does not follow the way of discipline and that true fellowship is brought about only by means of words and love. At the same time, these early ascetics believed that we all are paying our penalty, being exiled from paradise, and since we are guilty ourselves, we are not competent to judge and punish others. Only God is competent to do this. This idea serves to differentiate the eremitical and cenobitical monasticism. Basil would not agree with this point of view. He believed that it is a person's duty towards one's brother not to allow him to stray from the path of righteousness. A person should warn his brother and try to correct him.[90] None of the great leaders in the desert would have agreed with Basil.[91]

But as time passed, the hermits came to realize that cenobitic life had different laws from those of the cell and they accepted that an abbot should instruct those who disobeyed orders and neglected their duty, but he should do this with those who were directly subordinated to him, and not with others who were "outside" his monastery.[92]

II. Rewards

Though the hermits and the cenobites had two different standpoints regarding questions of punishment, they agreed fully on the question of rewards. Both hermits and cenobites were very parsimonious in rewarding their disciples. The reason was that they considered praise and every kind of reward as the cause of evil, since these things encourage pride. Monks wanted to avoid pride in any form, since it was the cause of the first fall. For this reason, Ascetic Literature warns monks to be very careful of those who honor and praise them.[93] John Climacus says that God hides from our eyes those perfections that we have obtained, and he adds that

> "... he who praises us or rather misleads us, opens our eyes by his praise, and as soon as our eyes are opened our treasure vanishes."[94]

Moreover, the Desert Fathers could not see any reason for praising someone since whatever good he possesses is God's gift. And it is shameful to be praised and proud of the adornments of others. But at the same time, the Desert Fathers did not avoid reminding their disciples of heavenly rewards in order to strengthen them in their laborious struggle for salvation.[95] However, monastic deontology made clear that a person who becomes a monk, fearing God's punishments or aiming at personal reward was a base Christian. The only motive which is fully accepted was love for God. Antony the "Father of Monasticism" had said: "I no longer fear God: I love Him." [96]

From what has been written, it can be seen that the Desert Fathers had a complete system of teaching methods, based on their theoretical ideas on education, especially on the principle of individualism. Most of the methods the Desert Fathers used originated from Greek sources but the Fathers modified, developed and adjusted them to their own needs and purposes.

Chapter V
Monks and Intellectual Culture

A. Their Attitude Towards Intellectual Culture

The term "intellectual culture" here includes every kind of activity related to books, mental and aesthetic development, and, in general, the sum of intellectual manifestations and achievements. Monasticism, and more generally Christianity, did not consider intellectual culture as a goal in itself since all worldy things are transient. Thus, monks renounced the world and its culture, accepting only those cultural elements which they thought might serve their purposes. Saints, rather than scholars, were the models of every monk. The early hermits in particular were suspicious of "worldly knowledge," which they believed was rooted in quite a different basic understanding of life. They were more concerned with forgetting the poetry, the philosophy, and, in general, the secular knowledge they had learned in schools before their conversion, than with further learning.[1] Antony was entirely illiterate. In his *Life* one reads:

> And again others such as these (philosophers) met him in the outer mountain and thought to mock him because he had not learned letters. And Antony said to them: "What say ye? Which is first, mind or letters? And which is the cause of which—mind of letters or letlers of mind?" And they answered "Mind is first and the inventor of letters." Antony said: "Whoever, therefore, hath a sound mind hath not need of letters." [2]

Monasticism in general regarded "letters" as a helpful means of attaining its goals. St. Pachomius, the first monastic legislator, embodied in his Rule his concern for the education of all his followers.[3] He commanded that the novice, before being accepted, should stay outside the door for several days and be taught how to read and write and learn by heart some part of the Scriptures, especially the Lord's Prayer, and as many psalms as he could learn.[4] After his entrance, the novice had also to learn the "ascetic alphabet" as it was believed to be of greater value for the monk.[5] One's free hours were supposed to be filled with readings from Scriptures which were often memorized. Such memorization was obligatory in the Pachomian monastery.[6] Early monasticism laid a strong emphasis upon the memorizing of the Psalter and the New Testament. Memorization was a common occupation of the early monks and a basic element of the ancient and medieval education. The Basilian Rule regarded it as a very good means of training novices.[7] This memorization was not a mechanical task, but an intellectual undertaking as is clear from St. John Cassian's *Institutions*:

> ... it is not the number of the verses that are repeated that must be our aim. Better to sing two verses with understanding than a whole Psalm with wandering thoughts.[8]

Even during meal-time there were to be readings to which brothers had to listen to intently so that their minds were in no way distracted by bodily pleasure; they were to rejoice in the Lord's words which, according to the 18th Psalm, were "sweeter than honey and the honey comb." This old custom still continues in both eastern and western monasteries.

Not only the sacred books, but also ordinary ones became inseparable companions for the monks. In the *Apophthegmata,* Palladius' *History,* and Theodoret's *History,* we find information about many book-loving monks.[9] In some cases, where poverty was applied in its strictest sense, an allowance was made for books. Alexander the Acemetos, for instance, allowed his Disciples to have books, although he blamed the monasteries for possessing even necessary utensils. In his *Life*, it is written that Alexander and his Disciples left for the Persian Desert "having nothing of the necessities of life, except the membranes where they had (written) the holy Scriptures." [10] A Syrian canon for nuns forbad visitors to give anything to the monastery, except a book.[11] When monks had read all the books they possessed, they usually borrowed more books from other monks. We possess a polite letter of a Coptic monk asking to borrow a book, which reads:

> "We greet your honoured pious paternity. Be so kind, if the thing pleases you, and do ye give us the book of Jesus (son) of Nauẽ. For they are writing for us (and) we find not a copy. Do the kindness with it. Farewell in the Lord our brethren Apa Daniel, John the priest Sona. From Thomas this humblest . . . [12]

Monasteries usually had their own libraries which they regarded as their armory. In the *Life* of St. Daniel, the Stylite, (409-493), one reads:

> For it is a custom in monasteries that many different books should be laid in front of the sanctuary and whichever book a brother wants he takes and reads.[13]

The monastic libraries did not contain only religious books, but many different kinds.[14] Especially during the Byzantine period, they were repositories of the ancient knowledge to which many had access. Men who had a love of learning, found monasteries to be the best places in which to fulfill their scholastic instincts and they were always welcomed by the monks. The famous Byzantine mathematician Leo (9th Century), for instance, journeyed to several monasteries in search of more knowledge. "When he found the right books, he immersed himself in them, and eventually attained great heights of education."[16] The monasteries were responsible for saving the relics of antiquity from the destructive mania of ignorance which began to take its toll in the fifth century. The monks provided a safe storage place for the records of the past.[17]

It is surprising that even St. Pachomius, the first monastic legislator, laid down rules protecting books and libraries. He wrote: "If someone takes a book and he does not take heed of it, but disdains it, let him make fifty prostrations."[18] Vööbus notes another interesting monastic canon which provides for the care of books:

> "Everyone who takes a codex to read or to collate and does not return it, or damages the copy, anathema will strike him, the leprosy of Gehazi on his soul and body, and the fate of Judas the traitor."[19]

This is a sample of the characteristic terminology in these devices of monastic librarianship which are not at all reminiscent of the practice of modern library science.

While the care taken of books preserved many manuscripts, a great many others were reproduced in the monastic scriptoria. According to Monastic tradition, the copying of manuscripts was regarded as a holy duty and monks and abbots participated in this work. Monastic records from different periods and places provide information concerning the copying of manuscripts. Palladius, describing the monastery of Pachomius, wrote that . . . their duties were in like fashion: One works on the land as a labour . . . another in the tannery . . . another in the scriptorium . . .[20]

The *Apophthegmata* mentions a certain monk Abraam who was a copy-writer. In one of his letters, Jerome talks about monks whose job was to copy manuscripts. Hierax the Anchorite, who lived during the first half of the fourth century, was a calligrapher and he continued writing until he died at the age of ninety.[21] In the *Life* of St. Marcellus and St. Melania we read that their duty was to copy books. Johannan's 'Ūrtaiā Disciples also were "... teachers and first-class scribes (and) these copied many books." [22] In a later period (9th-10th Century), in the Monastery of Studio, there existed "a school of writers" which had very strict rules for careless monks.[23] The record of monks who were copyists goes on. It is clear that the copying of manuscripts was a common duty of the early monks, and that love of learning moved the pens of these men. This love bequeathed to us what remains of Greek and Latin literature which otherwise would have disappeared as has the literature of Babylonia and Phoenicia.

The task of copying manuscripts was not merely a mechanical one either, but, like the memorizing of Scripture passages, it had an intellectual and moral effect. It was a holy function, as we have seen, and, for this reason, a prayer was employed in the blessing of the scriptorium:

> Vouchsafe, o Lord, to bless this scriptorium of Thy servants, and all that dwell therein, that whatsoever sacred writings shall be here read or written by them, they may receive with understanding and profit by the same, through our Lord Jesus Christ Amen. (8th Century) [24]

The work of copying was also laborious and complex. Some monks copied the text, others bound it, and others had to illustrate and ornament it. Finally, yet another monk had to go over it and correct any errors. All these tasks were done in the special room called the "Scriptorium."

Those monks, living an undistracted life in the quietness of the desert and having their attention turned towards their inner being, had many thoughts and feelings which had to be expressed in their letters to clergy and laymen who had asked for their advice, and in the books which they wrote. Their contribution to such field as literature, painting, music, architecture, the practical arts, was certainly noteworthy. It may be said that their achievements were among the finest of the human spirit.[25]

We have already mentioned Ephraem the Syrian and his contribution to Syriac letters. This monk has been described as the man "who stands without a rival in the rank of the most outstanding authors the Syrians can call their own." His 7-syllabus "mēmra," which was a didactic religious epic, or sermon, in metrical form, and his "Madrāsā," which was an artful lyric or didactic song, sung by a double chorus, raised his reputation so high that he is regarded as a better poet than his teacher Aswānā and a significant example "of the early symbiosis between monastic and literary life."[26] The work of these first pioneers was continued by later monks, such as Romanos (6th Century), the greatest hymn-writer of the early Church, St. Andrew of Crete (7th Century), who in his "Great Canon" introduced a new type of Church Poetry, St. John of Damascus (7th-8th Century), St. Cosmas of Maiuma (8th Century), and, later, by the Studites (9th Century).

B. Monastic Schools

Eastern monasticism, always a center of asceticism and mysticism, never intended that monasteries should become homes of study, but that they should remain as places of inner "quies." Their aim was not to influence the world, but to escape from it. However, at an early stage, monasticism ascertained the scholarly side of Christianity and developed a good relationship with "letters" as has already been shown. Pachomius wanted all his brothers to be able to read and know by heart the Psalms and parts of the New Testament. People not knowledgeable in these things were to be given lessons by one of the monks as we have already seen. These educational activities of early monasticism later led to the monastic schools for children which appeared in the

4th century and played a very important role in medieval western Europe.

In the Eastern Church, the acceptance of children into the monasteries was a disputed question, which troubled Eastern Monasticism for centuries. The early hermits and the regulations of many later monasteries were opposed to the acceptance of the children and they forbade monks to undertake their education.[27] Nevertheless, St. Pachomius and others had adopted children who were treated like novices who were placed in the charge of the older monks who were their spiritual fathers. The monks taught spiritual rather than intellectual matters. Basil also allowed children to enter the monasteries and he established the teaching system. Yet Basil, after a certain amount of hesitation, even allowed children, who did not intend to enter the ranks of monasticism—("children of the world")—to attend the lessons given by the monks, if their parents wanted to send them there.[28] He regarded monasteries as the ideal place for schools since they were in quiet locations. He determined in his Rule that special buildings for the use of the school were to be constructed. Chrysostom also was in favor of monastic schools as has already been said.[29]

It seems that about the end of the fourth century some monastic schools did exist. Chrysostom had attended such a school in the area of Antioch. St. Jerome also had such a school for Roman boys in Bethlehem, where grammar, Virgil and other poets and history were taught.[30]

Some years after Basil's death the fourth Ecumenical Council (451), gave permission (by its 3rd Canon), to clergy and monks to become the guardians of "those not yet come of age." Thus orphanages for both sexes and schools for children who had been gathered around the monks, were canonically associated with Basilian and other monasteries. In some cases not only children but even adults were attending monastic schools.

With regard to the curriculum and methods of the

monastic schools, there is not enough information from monastic sources. From Basil's Rule and other writings, one can form a very faint picture, although there was not any uniformity among the existing schools.

Basil, agreeing with Plato's and Aristotle's ideas,[31] says that the child should start his schooling at the age of seven. Children began learning the alphabet by copying their teacher who wrote the shape of the letter, while pronouncing it aloud. The sloping way of writing was forbidden as it was thought to be indecent.[32]

The Holy Scriptures, especially the Psalms, were used as reading texts because of their pleasant character. Isidorus of Pelusium recommended the Proverbs of Solomon which Basil also found to be useful.[33]

According to Basil, monastic schools were to teach history, which Basil regarded as a very important subject, and biology.[34] Music was also thought to have a beneficial influence upon children, and in general upon those "who are youthful in disposition."[35] Chrysostom also underlines the usefulness of sacred melody. According to St. Basil, music was to be taught with the use of an instrument called the Psalterion. The organ flute was excluded from use in the schools, for it was believed to arouse the passions.[36] This thought is also found in Aristotle's *Politica* IX.6. Basil was not very favorable towards mathematics and astronomy. Physical education was not included in the curriculum since it was considered to be of very little use, though Basil lamented the closing of the Gymnasium of his city.[37] Among the practical arts, the pupils in monastic schools were to be taught agriculture, building, weaving, working leather and brass, and other useful skills.[38]

Basil recommends[39] teachers to be explicit and brief, to use simple language and to avoid abstract meanings and allegoric interpretation of subjects. Teaching was to be done in a supervisory way, starting from the simplest elements. With regard to the teacher, Basil[40] wanted him to be well matured in age, experienced, and imposing since a presupposition for learning was the students' respect for and trust in their teacher. Yet he wanted the teacher to be pious, humble, and even tempered.

Finally, it must be said that, in early Byzantine times, monastic schools had a limited influence both because of their small number and because of the fact that they were more for the education of those who intended to enter monasticism rather than for children who would remain outside monasticism. Thus, these schools were intended for the education of persons within the bounding of monasticism for the most part.

In summary, it can be said that monks were favorably disposed towards intellectual culture inasmuch as it promoted their aims. At the same time, they made a valuable contribution to literature and the fine arts. Von Harnack commented on them by saying that, whatever is beautiful, comes from those who have renounced the world. Arts, poetry, and science were served by them. The principles of our civilization are part of the history of the monastic life,[41] but this contribution to civilization was, to some extent, accidental. A monk, for example never aimed at writing a poem; he wanted instead to receive God's mercy, so, he wrote a prayer; or he wanted to paint an icon for devotional purposes and not for artistic reasons. We regard these products as pieces of fine art and literature, but the monks regarded them simply as a means of fulfilling their goals. Monasticism never intended to produce artists and scholars, just saints, and it was to a remarkable degree successful.[42]

Epilogue

Reviewing what has been discussed in the previous chapters it is worth bearing in mind that the Early Church Fathers were quite aware of many of the main questions concerning Education and that they had their own personal ideas on them. Therefore, they regarded Heredity and Environment as two powerful factors influencing a person's development and they introduced a third factor, Divine Grace, which stood above the other two.

Starting from this basis, the Fathers took for granted that a person could be educated. A number of teaching methods were suggested and used by the Early Fathers which apply mainly to monastic Education. The variety of teaching methods was due to their belief that every individual has his own personality which was different in many ways from that of others and which required a special method of teaching for its best development. No one method was applicable to all people. Punishments also were to be chosen according to the individuality of the offender and to the nature of the crime. Further, the Early Church Fathers had a clear idea of the kind of nature which the teacher of a novice and, indeed, any school teacher should possess. Regarding Education as a very hard task, they wanted the school teacher to have a great amount of experiences, and certain personal qualities. An inexperienced teacher and one who lacked the necessary qualifications, was regarded as a harmful person. Furthermore, it can be said that, although most of the Early Fathers studied in the present work were mainly monks and had no intention of becoming educators, they applied themselves to certain intense educational activities. Education for them was not a goal in itself, but was an extremely helpful means to reach their goal which was the Kingdom of Heaven. As teachers they felt that they were responsible for their followers whom they called "students" and "disciples." The disciples called their elders "fathers" and "teachers" as well and they looked to them with trust, imitating their examples and looking forward to their teaching. In many cases, even faithful laymen went to famous masters of the desert for counselling and spiritual advice and they accepted them as great teachers.

The Early Fathers, as instructors, did not teach their followers "letters," or any other art, but a way of life; yet in some cases, they taught the novices, children, and adults "letters" and other secular knowledge, not for the sake of knowledge, but in order to make their disciples able to read and understand the Scriptures.

It is obvious, then, that the Early Fathers as a group were Educators. It should be understood that not every monk had all of the necessary credentials as educator; yet those who had the credentials were the most outstanding figures of the desert. A good number of monks remained in the ranks of the disciples during their entire lives, although, from a certain point of view, even disciples shared in the education of their elders and their colleagues.

As Educators, the Early Fathers were pioneers to some extent, but most of their theoretical ideas and teaching methods have a Biblical, or ancient Greek, origin. Certainly they adjusted and improved whatever ideas they took from other sources in order that they might suit their system and serve their purposes better. At the same time, the Early Fathers were among the earliest Educators who emphasized sufficiently the principle of individualized education and the need of a supervised way of teaching. In the ascetic writings, one finds many other interesting comments on education and the seeds of some modern ideas. The message, which the Early Fathers proclaimed to later generations, was the deep affection for the disciple and the absolute devotion to their educational duties. This message found many imitators, such as H. Pestalozzi and others.

Therefore, without any doubt, the Early Church Fathers form a powerful and characteristic body of educators who, in many respects, differ from the other "educators." Due to unceasing educational efforts, some of them, namely the Desert Fathers; have justly earned the title "professors of the desert." Others, namely, the "Three Hierarches," which included Basil the Great, Gregory the Theologian, and John Chrysostom, have been given the title "Ecumenical Doctors," and since 1842, they have been proclaimed as the patron saints of the Greek schools.

Appendix

The Story of Paul the Simple

The following story is found in Palladius' *Historia Lausiaca* (PG. 34, 1076-1084), It is a good illustration of the early monastic spirit and a characteristic specimen of the early ascetic literature.

The holy servant of Christ Hierax and Cronius and some other brothers, about whom I shall speak, were saying that a certain Paul, a country man, exceedingly guileless and simple in his manners, was wedded to a most beautiful woman of depraved character, who, for a long time escaping his notice, was sinning. However, he came home suddenly from the farm and found them (his wife and her lover) acting shamefully. Providence thus directed Paul to do what was beneficial for him. Seeing her with her lover, he laughed a little and called to them and said: "Good, good, truly I do not mind it. By Jesus, I will not take her any more. Go, you have her and her children, for I will go to become a monk." And saying nothing to anyone, he hastened to the blessed Antony and knocked at the door. Antony coming out, asked him: "What do you want?" Paul said to him: "I want to become a monk." Antony answered him and said: "A sixty-year-old man cannot become a monk here; but rather go to a town and work and live an active life giving thanks to God. For you cannot stand the afflictions of the desert." The old man answered again and said: "Whatever you teach me, I will do it." Antony said to him: "I have told you that you are an old man and you cannot become a monk; if you really want to become a monk, go and get into a cenobium with many brothers who can support your weakness. For I live here alone eating every fifth day and that not satisfying my hunger." With these and similar words, he scared Paul away. And since he could not stand him, Antony shut the door and did not come out for three days because of him, not even for his physical necessities.

Paul, however, did not go away, but stayed there. On the fourth day, however, necessity compelling him, he opened the door and came out. And seeing him again, he said to him: "Go away from here, old man, why do you distress me? You cannot stay here." Paul said to him: "It is impossible for me to die elsewhere than here." Having looked around, Antony saw that he did not have with him any food, neither bread, nor water, nor anything else, and that he was now for four days fasting. The great Antony thought he might die, being inexperienced in fasting, (and he said to himself): "I might stain my soul," so he received him. Antony said to him: "You can be saved; would you do whatever you hear from me?" Paul answered saying: "I will do everything you command."

Antony adopted in those days such a hard way of life, he had never tried even in the beginning of his youth. Testing his will, Antony said to him: "Stand and pray in this place until I will give you a work to do." And having gone inside the cave, he observed him through an opening being unmoved in that place the whole week, though he was burnt by the heat. And having moistened some palm-leaves, he said to him. "Take these, weave them into mats, as you see me doing." The old man wove until the ninth hour, completing fifteen times the length of the outstretched arms [equaling 90 feet] with much labor. Antony, having seen the woven palmleaves was displeased and assaulting him, he said: "You did not weave well, unweave them and weave them again." He imposed such a labor upon him, though he was in his fourth day of his fasting, and aged, so that he might be disgusted and flee from Antony and the monastic life. But he both unpicked them and wove again the same leaves, though it was more difficult, because they were wrinkled from the first weaving.

Therefore, the great Antony seeing that the old man neither murmured nor was discouraged nor angry, and that he did not turn his face at all, he felt compassion and at the sunset he said to him: "Papa, would you like us to eat a piece of bread?" Paul said to him: "As you think, abba." And this again moved Antony, that he did not rush towards eagerly at the announcement of the meal, but he had given him the authority to choose. "Set up the table," said Antony to the old man, and he obeyed.

Antony brought (a loaf of) bread and put on the table four biscuits, weighing about six ounces each. He moistened one for himself—for they were dry—and three for him. Then Antony started a psalm which he knew and, after singing it twelve times, he prayed twelve times to test Paul even in that as well. But the old man eagerly prayed with the great one. For he would have preferred to tend scorpions, so I think, to living with an adulterous woman. . . . After the twelve prayers, he said to him: "Come and take from the food." But after he laid the table and the food, he said: "Sit down and eat not until evening, but look only at the provisions." After evening had come and Paul had not eaten, Antony said to him: "Stand up and pray and then sit down." He, leaving the table, did in that way.

At midnight, he woke him up for prayer, extending the prayers until the ninth hour of the (next) day. Setting up the table again, he ordered him to take from the food and they sat down to eat late in the evening. Antony, having eaten the one biscuit, he did not touch another. But the old man, eating more slowly, was still at the little biscuit he started. Antony was waiting for him to finish and he said to him: "Papa, eat another biscuit." Paul said to him: "If you will eat, I will too; if you do not eat, I will not eat." Antony said to him: "I have had enough; for I am a monk." Paul replied to the great one: "I too have had enough, for I want to become a monk." They rose again and he said twelve prayers and sang twelve psalms. And after the prayers, they slept a little of the first sleep and again they woke up to chant at midnight until day.

Then he sent him away to wander in the desert saying: "Come back after three days." After this had been done, and some brothers had come to Antony, Paul was paying attention to Antony, what he might ask him to do. Antony said to him: "Serve the brothers silently and do not eat anything before the brothers are gone." When then the three weeks passed and Paul had not eaten anything, the brothers asked him: "Why are you silent?" Paul did not answer and Antony said to him: "Why are you silent? Talk to the brothers." Then he spoke.

Another time, when a jar full of honey was brought to Antony, he said to Paul: "Break the pot and let the honey be poured out." So he did. Then Antony said to him: "Amass the upper part of the (poured) honey without (amassing) any dirt." And again he ordered him to pump water every single day. Antony, having torn Paul's garment, ordered him to sew it, and Paul sewed it. And the man acquired so much obedience that the gift of banishing the demons was given to him from God. So, when Antony saw that the old man had eagerly followed him in his ascetic way of life, he said to him: "Behold, brother, if you can do thus every day, stay with me." Paul said him: "If there is anything more you will show to me, I do not know; for I can do easily those things I have seen you doing." Then, the following day, Antony said to him: "Behold, in the name of the Lord, you have become a monk."

So the great and blessed Antony, having been very

much convinced that the servant of Christ, Paul, was a very perfect soul, being very simple, after the required months—God's grace co-operating with the blessed Antony—he made him a cell, three or four miles from his own cell. And Antony said to him: "Behold, with Christ's help, you have become a monk; remain alone in order that you may experience (the attacks of) the demons." The simple Paul dwelt alone for a year and he was deemed worthy of grace over demons and all kinds of diseases and achieved to a full degree the virtue of ascetic life.

One day, a young man, who was very much possessed by demons, was brought to blessed Antony. He was possessed by a chief-demon, who cursed even heaven itself. So Antony, having examined the young man, said to those who brought him: "This is not my task. For the power over the chief-rank of demons has not yet been granted to me, but this is the gift of Paul the simple." So the blessed Antony went off and led them to the excellent Paul and said to him: "Abba Paul, cast out this demon from the man, that he may go away cured to his own, and glorify the Lord." Paul said to him: "Why not you?" Antony said to him: "I have not time, I have another work." And Antony left the youth there and went back again to his own cell.

So the guileless old man rose up and having prayed an effective prayer, addressed the demoniac and said: "Abba Antony has said go out from the man in order that he may be cured and glorify the Lord." But the demon cried out with blasphemy: "I am not coming out, greedy and bad old man." So Paul took his own sheep-skin coat and struck him on his back saying: "Go out, Abba Antony has said it." But the demon abused more both Antony and Paul saying: "What is in common between you and us, greedy, forgetful and avid men, who never mind your own business; why are you torturing us?" Finally, Paul said to him: "You are going out; or else I will go and tell Christ. By Jesus, if you do not go out, I am going right now to tell Christ, alas to you, what he would do to you." The wild demon defamed even Christ, saying: "I am not coming out."

Because of that, the holy Paul got angry with the demon and went away from his place at high noon. The heat of the Egyptians, especially that in those places, is similar to the furnace of Babylonia (Dan. iii). And standing on a rock on the mountain, like a pillar, he who was the pillar of heaven, prayed saying: "You see, O Jesus Christ, who was crucified under Pontius Pilate, that I will not descend from the rock, I will not eat, I will not drink, until I die, unless you hear now (my prayer) and cast out this demon from the man, and free him from this evil spirit." The simple and humble Paul still speaking to Christ, the demon cried out, before Paul had finished his words: "I am going, I am going, I am driven away by violence and tyranny. I am departing from the man, I will not touch him again. The humility and simplicity of Paul drive me away, and where am I to go I do not know." And immediately, the spirit of the demon went out and was turned into a great dragon seventy cubits long. And creeping, went away to the Red Sea, that the saying might be fulfilled; "The righteous will declare the faith that is shown." (Prov. XI), and again in another: "But to this man will I look, even to him that is poor and of a contrite spirit and trembles at my word." (Isa. XVI). For it is a custom that the lowest of demons are to be driven out by those men who are first in faith and that the chief-demons are to be chased out by the humble ones.

These are the miracles of the simple and humble one, and many others, greater than these. He was surnamed "Simple" by all the brotherhood.

Footnotes to the Introduction *

1. F. Woodhouse, *Monasticism: Ancient and Modern*, p. 2.

2. In his book, *Die Protestantische Thebais*, Ernst Benz demonstrates clearly that the works attributed to Macarius the Egyptian, written by an unknown fifth (?) century ascetic, created a mystic and pietistic movement in Germany, West Europe and America during the 17th and 18th century.

The monastic spirit was also a very important element of Russian culture, as it is evident Dostoyevsky's writings. In his book *The Brothers Karamazov* he pictures staretz Ambrose as the staretz Zosima, who had directed many eminent Russians. The Russian word "staretz" means "an old wise man," and it is used with reference to the elders of a monastery.

3. Matthew 19:12.

4. I Corinthians 7:29-34.

5. Matthew 19:21.

6. Romans 6:8, Galatians 5, Colossians 3, II Corinthians 4, Titus 2:12.

7. Matthew 4:17

8. *Bios Pachomiou*, V.H.P. XL, p. 129.

9. J. Hannay, *The Spirit and the Origin of Christian Monasticism*, p. 108.

10. O. Chadwick, *John Cassian*, pp. 51-52

11. Jerome, *Illustrious Men*, II, P.N.F., II, p. 365

12. Hebrews 13:14.

13. Tertullian, *Apology*, 38, 3, P.L., 1, 52B

14. Eusebius, *Historia Ecclesiastica*, 6.42, P.G. 20,613A

15. *Apophthegmata*, P.G. 65, 277B.

AUTHOR'S NOTE: All translations from Greek and Latin are mine, unless otherwise stated. I want to thank Dr. Eric Segelberg who has followed my work with great interest and has always been ready to let me profit by his great knowledge and versatility. Thanks must also go to Dr. R. Allen, Mr. J. Mann, M.A., and Dr. G. Schaus for their assistance in proof reading.

16. *Bios Pachomiou*, V.H.P., XL, p. 199.

17. D. Chitty, *The Desert A City*, p. 7.

18. J. Hannay, *The Spirit and the Origin of Christian Monasticism*, p. 109.

19. H. Workman, *The Evolution of Monastic Ideal*, p. 10.

20. K. Kirk, *The Vision of God* (London: 1941), p. 117.

21. See the 4th canon of the Fourth Synod of Chalcedon (451 A.D.).

22. Neo-Platonism, for instance, offered a ready-made system of thought that was in many ways in agreement with the monastic understanding of the reality: it was theocentic, contemplative, with not much appreciation for the tangible. Moreover, Christians of some sort of Stoic and Cynic backgrounds might have been encouraged to renounce bodily pleasures and society. The majority, however, of the monks were simple people seeking union with Christ in His passion, and were not contemplating philosophers.

23. Matthew 7:14.

24. Athanasius, *Vita Antonii* (The Life of St. Antony), P.G. 26, 884.

25. Athanasius, *Vita Antonii*, P.G. 26, 915.

26. Athanasius, *Vita Antonii*, P.G. 26, 865, tr. D. Chitty, *The Desert a City*, p. 5.

27. Palladius, *Historia Lausiaca*, P.G. 34, 1020.

28. E. Morrison, *Basil and his Rule*, p. 40.

29. Sozomenus, *Historia Ecclesiastica*, P.G. 67, 1396.

30. P. Brown, *The World of Late Antiquity*, p. 96.

Footnotes to Chapter 1

1. Justin the Martyr, *Apology*, II, 13, A.N.F., I, p. 193.

2. Justin the Martyr, *Apology*, I, 46, P.G. 6, 39.

3. Clement of Alexandria, *Paedagogus*, II.2, V.H.P., 7, p. 214. Philo of Alexandria, an older contemporary of St. Paul, had previously worked along these lines. His influence on Christian thinkers was very important, but had little influence on Jewish thought. See H. Chadwick, "Philo and the Beginnings of Christian Thought," *The Cambridge History*, ed. A. H. Armstrong.

4. J. Quasten, *Patrology*, II, p. 37.

5. P. Monroe, *History of Education*, p. 222.

6. W. Jaeger, *Two Rediscovered Works of Ancient Christian Literature: Gregory of Nyssa and Macarius* (Leiden: 1954) p. 34.

7. Basil, *Quod Mundanis . . .* , P.G. 31, 563-590.
8. Basil, *Letter to Libanius*, P.N.F., VIII, p. 325.
9. W. Jeager, *Early Christianity and Greek Paideia*, p. 82.
10. J. Quasten, *Patrology*, III, p. 203.
11. Tertullian, Against Heretics, 7, A.N.F., III, p. 246.
12. *Didascalia Apostolorum*, ed. Fr. Funk, II. p. 51.
13. Tertullian, *Against Heretics*, VII, A.N.F., III, p. 246.

Until the fourth century A.D. Middle-Platonism had been the predominant Greek philosophy. Later Neo-Platonism became an influential school. Both schools exercized a great influence upon the Christian thought. Stoic ethics also had a considerable influence on Christian morality. The Aristotelian influence was very limited in the beginning. Much of Stoicism and Aristotelianism was introduced to Christianity through Stoicized and Aristotelianized Platonism. From the sixth century and onwards the influence of the Aristotelian logic is considerable. In the 13th a kind of Aristotelian philosophy was introduced into Latin philosophical theology by Thomas Aquinas, and Aristotle became its basis ever since. Epicureanism and the agnostic views of the Sceptics could not influence Christianity in any way. Finally, as indicated by A. H. Armstrong, Christianity has to some extent influenced Neo-Platonic thought of the fifth and the sixth century. Prof. Armstrong gives a comprehensive and well balanced account of Greek philosophical influence on Christianity during the first five centuries A.D. (See A. H. Armstrong, "Greek Philosophy and Christianity," in the new *Legacy of Greece*, ed. M.I. Finley, to be published shortly by Oxford University Press).

14. H. Marrou, *A History of Education in Antiquity*, p. 422.
15. E. Power, *History of Education*, p. 200.
16. Chrysostom, quoted by E. Power, *History of Education*, p. 230.
17. Theodoret, *Historia Religiosa*, IV. 15, P.G. 82, 1157.
18. P. McCormick, *History of Education*, p. 214.
19. Balsamon, *Canonical Questions*, P.G. 138, 978.
20. Gr. Dix, *The Treatise on the Apostolic Tradition of St. Hippolytus*, 2nd ed. (London: 1968), p. 25.
21. *Vie d'Alexandre l'Acémète*, II. 22, P.O.R., VI, p. 673.
22. Ephesians 6:4.
23. Clement of Rome, *Letter to Corinthians*, 21, P.G. 1, 257.
24. Ignatius, *Epistula ad Philadelphios*, 4, P.G. 5, 825.

25. Fr. Eby, *History of Education*, p. 602.
Heretics, XXXVIII, A.N.F., I, 519.

27. Eusebius, *Apologetica*, 12.60, P.G. 21, 985 and 988.

28. "Constitutiones Apostolorum," 8.32, ed. Fr. Funk, *Didascalia Apostolorum*, p. 175.

29. L. Sherril, *The Rise of Christian Education*, pp. 175, 184 and 192.

30. Eusebius, *Historia Ecclesiastica*, VI.29/IV.15, P.G. 20, 582 and 533. See also Jerome, *Lives of Illustrius Men*, 38, P.N.F., IV, p. 371.

31. Eusebius, *Historia Ecclesiastica*, VI.18, F.T.C., XXIX, p. 33.

32. Ch. Cruttwell, *A Literary History of Early Christianity*, (London: 1893), p. 430.

33. A. Voobus, *History of Asceticism in the Christian Orient*, p. 413.

Footnotes to Chapter II

1. John Climacus, *Ladder*, p. 206.

2. Macarius the Egyptian, *Homily LXXV*, V.H.P., XLII, 93.

The Eastern and Western Churches hold two differnet concepts of "original sin." The latter teaches that Adam's sin is inherited by his descendants who lack the freedom of choice. Adam had exercised it and sinned for the whole human race. The Eastern Church, however, understands the "original sin" as a kind of illness, which affects the whole of human nature, and leads to sin. Each individual, even in its fallen state, preserves its freedom, and is totally responsible for its actions. Each man repeats and imitates Adam's fault, but does not partake in its guilt. In other words, according to the Western Church, Adam has sinned on behalf of all mankind, but according to the Eastern Church, every man is the "Adam" of his soul. (See H. W. Robinson, *The Christian Doctrine of Man*, p. 171, and J. Meyendorff, *Christ in Eastern Christian Thought*, p. 117)

3. Romans 7:23.

4. Gregory of Nazianzus, *Oration II,2,* P.N.F. VII, 207.

5. Macarius the Egyptian, *Homily XXVII, 10,* V.H.P. XLI, 286.

6. Clement of Alexandria, *Paedagogus*, II.10, V.H.P., VII, p. 169.

7. John Climacus, *Ladder XXV*, p. 188, See also Macarius the Egyptian, *Homily XV*, V.H.P., XLI, 230, and Ireaeus, *Against Heretics, XXXVIII*, A.N.f., I, 519.

8. Palladius, *Historia Lausiaca, XCV*, P.G. 34, 1201. John Climacus, *Ladder, XXV*, p. 180.

9. Basil, *Hexaemeron, Homily IX, 4,* N.P.F., VIII, 103.

10. Macarius the Egyptian, *Homily LIV*, V.H.P. XLII, 42.

11. Clement of Alexandria, *Stromata*, VI.11 and 12, V.H.P., VIII, p. 213-4.

12. Marcarius the Egyptian *Letter*, V.H.P., XLII, p. 146.

13. G. Ralles, *Syntagma Kanonon*, IV, p. 341.

14. John Climacus, *Ladder*, XXVIII, p. 189 and 206.

15. *Apophthegmata*, V.H.P., XLII, 256.

16. *Apophthegmata*, P.G. LXV, 77, 116, 361. See also *Constitution of Holy Apostles*, Bk. V, 2, A.N.F. I, p. 438, *and* Ammonas, *Letter III*, V.H.P. XL, 52.

17. *Vita Prima Pachomii*, quote, in Chitty's *The Desert a City*, p. 21.

18. Chrysostom, *De Anna, Sermo III*, 2, P.G. 54, 655A.

19. John 15:5.

20. Macarius the Egyptian, *Letter*, V.H.P., XLII, p. 146.

21. Dobzhansky, Th., *Heredity and Nature of Man*, p. 4.

22. *Apophthegmata*, P.G. 65, 281.

23. Clement of Alexandria, *Instructor, I, 12*, A.N.F., II, 235. See also Macarius the Egyptian, *Ascetic Homily*, V.H.P., XLII, p. 188 and John Climacus, *Klimax*, 11, p. 78.

24. *Varsanuphius and John*, Question XIII, P.O.R. XXXI, Fsc 3, 469. See also Isidorus of Pelusium, *Letters, Bk. I*, P.G. 78, 425 B. and Macarius the Egyptian, *Ascetic Homily*, V.H.P., XLII, p. 221.

25. Basil, *Reg. Fus., XV*, P.G. 31, 956A.

26. John Climacus, *Klimax*, XXVI, p. 148.

27. John Climacus, *Ladder, XXVI*, p. 206.

28. Chrysostom, *Homilia, LXVIII, 3,* in Mt., P.G. 58, 643 D. See also D. Chitty, *The Desert a City*, p. 16, *and* W. Jaeger, *Early Christianity and Greek Paideia*, p. 99.

29. Athanasius of Alexandria, *Vita Antonii, L,* P.G. 26, 917C and 825C

30. Diadochus of Photices, (451 A.D.), *On Spiritual Perfection*, 54. See also Palladius, *Historia Lausiaca*, P.G. 34, 1003.

31. Matthew 19:12, I Corinthians 7:29, Romans 6:8, Titus 2:12, Galatians 5.

32. *Didache VIII*, V.H. P., II, p. 217-18.

33. Ignatius, *Letter to Polycarpus, II*, ed. K. Bihlmeyer, *Die Apostolischen Väter*, p. 112. See also Clement of Rome, *2nd Letter to Corinthians 12:6*, ed. K. Bihlmeyer, *Die Apostolischen Väter*, p. 76.

34. Maximus Confessor, *Capitum de Charitate*, P.G. 90, 1001B.

35. Basil, *Constitutiones*, P.G. 31, 1388A.

36. Athanasius, *Vita Antonii*, P.G. 26, 632A, and 889A. See also Palladius, *Vita Chrysostomi*, P.G. 47, 39, *and Apophthegmata*, P.G. 65, 1160.

37. John Climacus, *Ladder I*, p. 50.

38. *Apophthegmata*, V. H. P. XLII, 269.

39. *Apophthegmata*, P.G. 65, 257.

40. Ammonas, *Peri Psyches*, V.H.P., XL, 272 and *4th Letter*, V.H.P., XL, p. 54. See also Basil, *Commentaries on Isaias*, P.G. 30, 200B.

41. *Apophthegmata*, P.G. 65, 204A.

42. *Apophthegmata*, P.G. 65, 425C. See also Isidorus of Pelusium, *Epistolorum Libr. I62, 258*, P.G. 78, 292A.

43. *Apophthegmata*, P.G. 65, 368A.

44. Palladius, *Lausiac History*, ed. W. Clarke, p. 49. Morrison, E., *Basil and his Rule*, p. 79.

45. Basil, *Reg. Brev. 92*, P.G. 31, 1145 C.________ *Reg. Fus. P.G.* 31, 965B. Dualism is the doctrine which divides reality into two distinct realms: a higher, rational and divine realm, and a lower, irrational and material. In the same way man is divided into two unrelated parts: the soul, which is rational, immortal and of divine origins, and the body, which is material, mortal, impure, and the source of all sin and wickedness. This was a Greek and Eastern view of reality, but is not found in the Bible.

46. *Apophthegmata*, P.G. 65, 168 and 156.

47. *Varsanuphius and John*, Question 79, P.OR. XXXI, 559.

Footnotes to Chapter III

1. D. Chitty, "Some Lexicographical Notes," *Studia Patristica* III (1962), p. 263.

2. For the above terms see: *Apophthegmata*, P.G. 65, 73, 137, 153, 177, 256, 257 and 336. See also Palladius, *Historia Lausiaca*, P.G. 37, 1043 and 1081.

3. *Pachomius' Rule*, P.G. 40, 952 and 949.

4. Epiphanius of Cyprus, *Contra Haereses*, P.G. 42, 765.

________ *Panarion*, P.G. 41, 156. See also Basil, *Poenae in Monachos*, P.G. 31, 1309, and Palladius, *Historia Lausiaca*, P.G. 34, 1020 and 1068.

6. Basil, *Reg. Fus., XXXV*, P.G. 31, 1005C and 988A. See also Ephraem Syrus, *Opera Omnia*, pp. 323E, and 333E.

7. Ephraem Syrus, *Opera Omnia*, p. 79.

8. Isidorus of Pelusium, *Epistolarum Lib.*, P.G. 78, 345C. See also *Apophthegmata*, P.G. 65, pp. 117A, 195C, 196A.

9. John Cassian, *Institutions II, 5*, S. Chr. 109, pp. 60, 62, 63, 78, 168, 180, 268, 469.

10. Macarius of Egypt, *Homily LVIII*, V.H.P. XLII, 361.

11. John Climacus, *Ladder, I,* p. 51.

12. E. Budge, *Paradise II*, p. 161.

13. Gregory of Naz, *Oration LXXVII, 10*, P.N.F. VII, 207. See also Nilus the Ascetic, *Epistolarum Lib.*, P.G. 79, 758. and *Varsanuphius and John*, Question 13, P.OR. XXXI, 468.

14. Basil, *Reg. Fus.*, P.G. 31, 1029A, 1032, 988.

15. H. Percival, *The Seven Ecumenical Councils*, N.P.F. XIV, 231, See also *Apophthegmata*, P.G. 65, 188C.

16. *Apophthegmata*, P.G. 65, 203. See also *Varsanuphius and John*, Question 112, p. 597.

17. Gregory of Naz., *Oration XI*, P.N.F., VII, 214 and 37

18. Theodotus, *Excerpts*, A.N.F., VIII, 47.

19. John Climacus, *Klimax XXXI*, p. 177.

20. *Peri Pachomiou kai Theodorou*, V.H.P. XL, 193.

21. John Climacus, *Klimax XXXI*, p. 176.

22. *Varsanuphius and John*, Question 23, p. 480.

23. John Climacus, *Klimax XXXI*, p. 179 and 175

24. Basil, *Reg. Fus. XXX*, P.G. 31, 992-993.

25. *Life of St. Pachomius*, V.H.P., XL, 172.

26. John Moschus, *Leimon VII*, P.G. 87, pp. 111 and 2857.

27. *Varsanuphius and John*, Question 67, p. 539.

28. Basil, *Reg. Fus. XXV*, P.G. 31, 984C.

In his *Institutions*, Book IV. 30-31, Cassian mentions Abbot Pinufius, who left his large and famous monastery and out of humility and love of subjection went to a distant monastery where he could be received as a novice. When he was discovered he was brought back to his monastery. He stayed there for a little while and then he fled again into the region of Syrian Palestine.

29. *Vie d'Alexandre l'Acémète*, p. 689.

30. K. Kirk, *The Vision of God*, p. 86.

31. E. Budge, *Paradise II*, p. 3. Evagrius was a Neo-Platonic intellectual with a rich ascetic experience. He understood man as a fallen intellect, who should attempt to return to the state of purely intellectual activity. This was the state before the "fall." Evagrius was condemned, together with Origen, by the fifth Council of Constantinople, in 553 A.D.

32. *Apophthegmata*, P.G. 65, 245.

33. *Ibid.*

34. Palladius, *Vita Chrysostomi*, P.G. 47, 29. See also Nilus the Ascetic, *Epistula*, PG. 79, 557D and John Climacus, *Scala Paradisi*, P.G. 88, 1097B.

35. Athanasius of Alexandria, *Vita Antonii*, P.G. 26, 865, and Ephraem Syrus, *Opera Omnia*, p. 315.

36. Basil, *Epistula*, P.G. 32, 225B.

37. E. Morrison, *St. Basil and his Rule*, p. 52.

38. I. Hausherr, *John the Solitary* (Rome: 1939), p. 32.

39. John Climacus, *Ladder*, p. 19.

40. Nilus the Ascetic, *De Monachorum Praestantia*, P.G. 79, 1060A. See also Basil, *Reg. Brev. CXVI*, P.G. 31, pp. 1161B and 1161D.

41. O. Sumner, "*John Climacus,*" *The Guild of Pastoral Psychology*, No. 63, (London: 1950), pp. 14-15.

42. W. Nigg, Warriors of God, p. 52.

43. L. Lefort, *Saint Pachôme*, pp. 84-85.

44. John Cassian, Institutions, IV. 3-7, P.N.F., XI, p. 219ff.

45. Palladius, quote. in Chadwick's *John Cassian*, p. 11.

46. John Climacus, *Ladder*, p. 19. See also Macarius the Egyptian, *Letter*, V.H.P. XLII, 155.

47. In St. Antony's *Life*, (Chapters III-V), while Antony shows subjection to his teachers, there is no suggestion of formal acceptance of obedience to one spiritual father, but it seems that the bond was wholly voluntary.

48. John Climacus, *Ladder*, p. 69.

49. Clement of Alexandria, *Stromata II*, 23, P.G. 8, 1096.

50. E. Workman, *Evolution of Monastic Ideal*, p. 71.

51. C. Cary-Elwes, *Law, Liberty and Love*, p. 61.
52. Cyril of Alexandria, *Explanatio in Rom.*, P.G. 74, 789.
53. W. Crum, *Varia Coptica*, No. 6, p. 9.
54. *Histoire de St. Pachôme*, P.OR. IV, Fs. 5, No. 19, 434.
55. Th. Merton, *Contemplation*, p. 290.
56. I Corinthians 12:11.
57. Clement of Alexandria, *Stromata I, 1*, A.N.F., II, 30.
58. Isidorus of Pelusium, *Epistolarum Libr.*, P.G. 78, 1484.
59. John Climacus, *Ladder I*, p. 56.
60. John Climacus, *Klimax XXXI*, p. 117. and 180.
61. *Pachomius' Rule*, tr. G. Schodde. "The Rule of St. Pachomius," *Presbyterian Review*, (1885), p. 682.
62. Gennadius, *Lives of Illustrious Men*, P.N.F., III, 388.

Footnotes to Chapter IV

1. *Varsanuphius and John*, P.OR. XXXI, Fasc 3, 457.
2. Gregory of Naz., *Oration II, 30-32*, P.G. 35, pp. 437-438.
3. Clement of Alexandria, *Instructor*, ed. O. Stählin, I, 133.
4. John Climacus, *Klimax XXXI*, p. 174.
5. Mark 16:15, and Romans 10:14.
6. *Apophthegmata*, P.G. 65, pp. 188c, 232, 273, 405, 440.
7. Basil, *On the Spirit, XV*, P.N.F., VIII, 21.
8. Isidorus of Pelusium, *Epistola I, 441*, P.G. 78, 425B.
9. John Climacus, *Klimax XXXI*, p. 174.
10. Gregory of Nyssa, *Catechetica Magna*, P.G. 45, 10.
11. Gregory of Naz, *Oration II*, P.N.F. VII, 210.
12. *Entolai Pachomiou*, V.H.P. XL, 114.
13. *Vita Pachomii*, quoted in Chitty's *The Desert a City*, p. 26 and 25.
14. *Apophthegmata*, P.G. 65, pp. 81, 253, 303, 324, 325.
15. Ibid., p. 301D.
16. *Gerontikon*, p. 164b and 118b.
17. Basil, *Reg. Fus. XXV*, P.G. 31, 984C.
18. Palladius, *The Lausiac History*, ed. C. Bulter, (Cambridge, 1898), p. 234.
19. Basil, quoted in K. Mouratides' *Christokentrike Poimantike*, p. 68.
20. Ibid.
21. *Bios Pachomiou*, V.H.P. XL, pp. 176-178 and 180.

22. *Apophthegmata*, P.G. 65, pp. 208, 209, 333, 365-68.

23. Basil, *In Hexaemeron*, IX, 80, P.G. 29, 188B.

24. Isidorus of Pelusium, *Epistola, IV, 117*, P.G. 78, 1192B and 1124.

25. Ch. Cruttwell, *Literary History of Early Christianity*, p. 452.

26. John Climacus, *Ladder*, pp. 144 and 203.

27. Wallace-Hadrill, *Greek Patristic View of Nature*, p. 124.

28. Ammonas, *Letter V*, V.H.P. XL, 160.

29. Maximus Confessor, *Questions*, P.G. 90, 840B.

30. Dionysios Hareopagite, *De Ecclesiastica*, P.G. 3, 480A.

31. *Bios Pachomiou, VI*, V.H.P. XL, 132.

32. Bell, I., *Jews and Christians in Egypt*, Papyri 1920, 11, and 1922, 5 and 11.

33. Sozomen, *Historia Ecclesiastica III, 14*, P.G. 67, 1069. See also Chadwick, D., *John Cassian*, p. 56. A period of probation had already been introduced by the time of Pachomius.

34. O. Chadwick, *John Cassian*, p. 56. Evagrius of Pontus, well versed in Greek philosophy, wrote that the hood symbolizes the Saviour's Grace, which protects the "hegemonicon." This is a Stoic term developed by Christians and refers to the principal part of the soul, the intellect. It was generally assumed that its seat was in the heart, and not in the head as it is here assumed by Evagrius. Furthermore, he reports and explains the meaning of the other items of the monastic habit. (See Evagrius of Pontus, *Capita Practica*, P.G. 40,1220C)

35. Sozomen, *Historia Ecclesiastica III, 14*, P.G. 67, 1069-1072.

36. Dorotheos, *Doctrina I*, P.G. 88, 1632C-1636A.

37. Maximus Confessor, *Questiones*, P.G. 90, 840-841.

38. Dorotheus, *Doctrina I*, P.G. 88, 1632C-1636A. Dorotheus writes that he is quoting the *Apophthegmata*. In the existing Greek version of the *Apophthegmata* his reference regarding the "hegemonicon" is not found, but the wording of that paragraph is identical with that found in Evagrius, *Capita Practica*, P.G. 40, 1220C.

39. Sozomen, *Historia Ecclesiastica*, P.G. 67, 1072A.

40. *Apophthegamata*, P.G. 65, 373-376. This is probably a dramatization of the well known Aesopian fable.

41. Ibid., pp. 129, 121 and 181.

42. Ibid., pp. 100-101.

43. Evagrius of Pontus, *Capita Practica*, P.G. 40, 1249B.

44. Basil, *Hexaemeron*, P.N.F., VIII, 103, 106.
45. Cyril of Jerusalem, *Catechesis, IX, 13*, P.G. 33, 652B.
46. Ammonas, *Letter IV*, V.H.P. XK, 53.
47. *Apophthegmata*, P.G. 65, 420 and 173.
48. Ephraem Syrus, *Ascetic Works*, by Sakkoraphos, p. 22.
49. John Climacus, *Ladder XXVI*, p. 203.
50. Palladius, *Historia Lausiaca LII*, P.G. 34, 1138B. See also *Apophthegmata*, P.G. 65, 245A.
51. *Apophthegmata*, P.G. 65, 440A and 364C.
52. Ibid., p. 197 and 224.
53. *Gerontikon*, p. 114B.
54. *Apophthegmata*, P.G. 65, 337.
55. Basil, *Homilia in Psalmum 47*, P.G. 29, 457.
56. Gregory of Nyssa, *De Virginitate*, P.G. 46, 409-412.
57. Isidorus of Pelusium, *Epistola*, P.G. 78, 1537C. Nilus the Ascetic, *Homily*, Philokalia, I, p. 205 and 206.
58. Clement of Alexandria, *Stromata I, 1*, A.N.F. II, 300.
59. Br. Joyce, *Alternative Models of Elementary Education*, (Waltham, Mass.: 1969), p. 106f.
60. Ph. Jacob, *Changing Values in College* (N. York: 1956). See also C. Passakos, *Statherotes kai Metabolai eis Prosopikas Axias* (Athens: 1974), p. 130.
61. Basil, *Hexaemeros IX, 9*, P.N.F., VIII, 106.
62. Ephraem Syrus, *Ascetic Works*, ed. Sakkoraphos, p. 27.
63. Athanasius, *Vita Antonii LV*, V.H.P. XXXIII, 39.
64. *Vita Antonii*, quote in Wigg's *Warriors of God*, p. 39.
65. *Varsanuphius and John, Question LXXXV*, P.O.R. XXXI, 565.
66. John Climacus, *Ladder XXVII*, p. 239.
67. Athanasius, *Vita Antonii XIX*, P.G. 26, 872B. See also Ephraem Syrus, *Ascetic Works*, ed. Sakkoraphos, p. 25.
68. *Apophthegmata*, P.G. 65, 77.
69. Basil, *Reg. Fus., XXVI*, P.G. 31, 985.
70. *Apophthegmata*, P.G. 65, 201.
71. John Climacus, *Klimax*, p. 174.
72. John IV (ob. 715), Patriarch of Constantinople, *Poenitentiale*, P.G. 88, 1904A.
73. Basil, *Reg. Brev. LXXXI*, P.G. 31, 1140. See also K. Mouratides, *Christokentrike Poimantike*, p. 70.
74. *Apophthegmata*, P.G. 65, 325.
75. *Apophthegmata*, P.G. 65, 217-218 and 336.

76. Gregory of Naz, *Oration XVI*, P.N.F., VII, 253.

77. *Vita S. Marinae*, P.L. 73, 693.

78. Clement of Alexandria, *Instructor, I. 5*, A.N.F. II, 213. See also St. Cyprian, *Treatise on the Dress of Virgins*, A.N.F., V, 430. "Discipline the safeguard of hope, the bond of faith, the guide of the way of salvation, the stimuli and the nourishment of good dispositions, the teacher of virtue, causes us to abide always in Christ and to live continually for God, and to attain to the heavenly promises and to the divine rewards."

79. *Bios Pachomiou*, V.H.P., 40, 154. See also Clement of Alexandria, *Instructor II, 8*, A.N.F. II, 282.

80. Ammonas, *Parainetika*, V.H.P. XL, 64.

81. *Bios Pachomiou*, V.H.P., XL, 165.

82. Basil, *Reg. Brev.* P.G. 31, 1109D and 1165B.

83. Basil, *Reg. Fus XV*, P.G. 31, 1040-41 and 953.

84. Gregory of Nyssa, *Catechetica Magna*, P.G. 45, 24-25.

85. Basil, *Reg. Brev. XCI*, P.G. 31, 1140A.

86. Pachomius, *Epitimia*, V.H.P., XL, 127. See also John IV, Patriarch of Constantinople (6th Century), *Poenitentiale*, P.G. 88, 1893B.

87. *Peri Pachomiou*, V.H.P. XL, 194.

88. *Bios Pachomiou*, V.H.P. XL, 261-262.

89. *Apophthegmata*, P.G. 65, 121B, 284A. See also *Gerontikon*, p. 104b.

90. Basil, *Reg. Brev. III and IV*, P.G. 31, 1084 and *Reg. Fus., XXV*, P.G. 31, 984C.

91. *Apophthegmata*, P.G. 65, 328C, 352A.

92. Ibid., p. 305A. See also *Histoire de Saint Pacôme*, P.OR., Tome IV, Fasc. 5, No. 19, p. 510.

93. Ammonas, *Parainetika*, V.H.P. XL, 62. See also Symeon the New Theologian, *Practika*, Philokalia, III, 254.

94. John Climacus, *Ladder XXII*, p. 175 and 181.

95. Macarius the Egyptian, *Homily IV*, V.H.P., XLI, 159.

96. *Apophthegmata*, P.G. 65, 85C.

Footnotes to Chapter V

1. H. Marrou, *History of Education*, p. 439.

2. Athanasius, *Vita Antonii*, P.N.F. IV, 215.

3. *Pachomii Praecepta*, P.G. 40, 949A. See also O'Connor,

J., *Monasticism and Civilization*, p. 82.

4. *Pachomius' Rule*, quote. P. Monroe in *A Text Book in History of Education*, p. 256.

5. John Climacus, *Ladder XXVI*, p. 204. Here is an excellent alphabet for all:

(A) obedience
(B) fasting
(C) sackcloth
(D) ashes
(E) tears
(F) confession
(G) silence
(H) humility
(I) vigil
(J) courage
(K) cold
(L) toil
(M) hard work
(N) humiliation
(O) contrition
(P) forgetfulness of wrongs
(Q) brotherly love
(R) meekness
(S) simple and unquestioning faith
(T) freedom from worldly cares
(U) hateless hatred of parents
(V) detachment
(X) innocent simplicity
(Z) voluntary abasement

6. Palladius, *Historia Lausiaca* XL, P.G. 34, 1105B and 1034B. The seventh canon of the Pachomian Rule determined that a monk who neglected his reading was to be punished "in front of the altar." See Pachomius, *Regulae*, V.H.P. XL, 114.

7. Basil, *Reg. Brev., XCV*, P.G. 31, 1084C and *Reg. Brev., CCXXXV*, P.G. 31, 1240C.

8. John Cassian, quote. in Workman's *Evolution of Monastic Ideal*, p. 131.

9. *Gerontikon*, p. 118A. Palladius, *Historia Lausiaca*, P.G. 34, 1034B. Theodoretus, *Historia Religiosa XII*, P.G. 82, 1397.

In his *Institutions*, Book IV. 17, Cassian states that the custom of reading at meals is of Cappadocian, and not of Egyptian, origins. Indeed, the Pachomian Rule orders silence during the meals (V.H.P. 40, 124), while the *Shorter Rule* of St. Basil suggests reading at meals (P.G. 31, 1204A, question 180).

10. *Vie d'Alexandre l'Acémète*, P.OR. Tom. 6, FC5, No. 30, p. 693 and 682.

11. A. Vööbus, *History of Ascetism*, Tomus 17, p. 388.

12. *Varia Coptica*, ed. W. Crum, p. 32.

13. El. Dawes, "Life of St. Daniel," ed. Dawes, *Three Byzantine Saints*, p. 8.

14. A. Vööbus, *History of Asceticism*, Tomus 17, p. 389.

15. Vacalopoulos, *Origins of the Greek Nation*, p. 20.

16. Sp. Lambros, "A Few Words Concerning Slavs in the Peloponnese." *Hora*, May 5, 1874, pp. 5-6.

17. Er. Goodenough, *The Church in Roman Empire*, p. 116.

18. Pachomius, *Poenai*, V.H.P., XL, 128.

19. A. Vööbus, *History of Asceticism*, Tomus 17, p. 383 and 391.

20. Palladius, *Historia Lausiaca*, P.G. 34, 1105B.

21. Epiphanius of Salamis, *Contra Hereses II*, P.G. 42, 176. See also *Apophthegmata*, P.G. 65, 132.

22. A. Vööbus, *History of Asceticism*, p. 390.

23. J. Phytrakes, *Monks as Social Teachers* (Athens: 1950), p. 43.

24. J. O'Connor, *Monasticism and Civilization*, p. 113 and 122.

25. Fr. Eby, *History and Philosophy of Education*, p. 638.

26. A. Vööbus, *History of Asceticism*, Tomus 17, p. 394-395. See also Palladius, *Historia Lausiaca*, P.G. 34, 1209

27. Ph. Koukoules, *Bios Byzantinon*, I, 46.

28. Basil, *Reg. Fus., XV*, P.G. 31, 953. ——— *Reg. Brev., CCXCII*, P.G. 31, 1288B. ——— *Reg. Fus.*, P.G. 31, pp. 952, 953, 1041, 1288.

29. Chrysostom, *Adversus Oppugnatores, III*, P.G. 47, 380.

30. Rufinus, *Apology II, 8*, P.N.F. III, 464-465.

31. Plato, *The Laws Z, 796C*, ed. E. England, p. 60. Aristotle, *Politica H. A.*, ed. W. Ross, p. 251.

32. Basil, *Homilia in Psalmum LXXXIV*, P.G. 29, 493. ——— *Epistola*, P.G. 32, 872. ——— *Epistolae*, ed. J. Garnier (Paris: 1721), III, 452.

33. Basil, *Homilia in Psalmum I*, P.G. 29, 212. Isidorus of Pelusium, *Epistola*, P.G. 78, 1092. Basil, *Reg. Fus. XV*, P.G. 31, 953C.

34. Basil, *Homilia II in Hexaemeron*, ed. J. Garnier, I, 14. Basil, *Homilia VII in Hexaemeron*, ed. J. Garnier, I, 77.

35. Basil, *Homilia in Psalmos I*, P.G. 29, 212B.

Indeed, because the Holy Spirit knew that the human race was difficult to be led toward virtue, and because of our inclination toward pleasure, we were taking no care of the right way of living, what did He do? He has mingled the delight of the melody with the doctrines, so that we might receive without noticing it the benefit of the words, through the pleasantness and smoothness of the sound heard. . . . This is why He contrived for us these harmonius tunes of the Psalms, so that they who are Children in age, or even those who are very youthful in disposition might seem that they are singing but, in reality, become trained.

36. Basil, *Homilia in Psalmum XLVII*, P.G. 29, 436. ——— *Homilia in Psalmum I*, P.G. 29, 212-215.

37. Nilus the Ascetic, *De Monastica Exercitatione*, P.G. 79, 808.

38. Basil, *Reg. Fus. XXXVII*, P.G. 31, 1017.

39. Basil, *Scholium*, P.G. 36, 1205. ——— *De Baptismo II, 6*, ed. J. Garnier, II, 639. ——— *Homily IX to Hexaemeron*, ed. J. Garnier, I, 80. ——— *De Baptismo, II, 6*, ed. J. Garnier, I, 659.

40. Basil, *Reg. Fus., XV*, P.G. 31, 953. ——— *Homily to Isaiah*, ed. J. Garnier, I, 451. ——— *De Baptismo II*, J. Garnier, II, 657. ——— *Ascetic Homily*, ed. J. Garnier, II, 205.

41. A. Harnack, *Das Mönchthum seine Ideal und seine Geschichte*, I, p. 84-85.

42. Ed. Myers, *Education in the Perspective of History*, p. 169.

Bibliography

A. Primary Sources

The Acts of the Christian Martyrs, Texts and Translation by H. Musurillo (Oxford: Clarendon Press, 1972).

Ammonas, *Letters*, V.H.P. XL. (Athens: Apostolike Diakonia, 1970).

Apophthegmata: Greek text. a) P.G. 65, 76-440. b) P. Paschos, *Gerontikon*, (Athens: Astir, 1970). English tr. c) H. Waddell, *The Desert Fathers*, tr. from Latin. (London: Constable, 1936). d) E. A. W. Budge, *The Paradise of the Fathers II*, tr. from Syriac. (London: 1907).

Aristotle, *Politica*, ed. W. D. Ross, Oxonii, 1957.

Athanasius of Alexandria, *Vita Antonii*, P.G. 26, 835-976. English tr. R. T. Meyer, *Ancient Christian Writers*, 10, 1950.

Balsamon, *Opera (Canonica, Juridica, Dogmatica)*, P.G. 138.

Basil the Great, *Regulae Fusius*, P.G. 31, 905-1052.

——— *Regulae Brevius*, P.G. 31, 1051-1306.

——— *Ascetica Disciplina*, P.G. 31, 648.

——— *De Baptismo*, P.G. 31, 1513.

——— *Constitutiones Asceticae*, P.G. 31, 1321.

_______ *Homiliae in Psalmos*, P.G. 29, 209.

_______ *Homiliae in Hexaemeron*, P.G. 29, 4.

Bible, King James' Authorized Version.

Cassian, *Institutions*, Text and intr. Jean-Claude Guy, (Paris: Sources Chrétiennes, No. 109, 1965).

Clement of Alexandria. *Paedagogus*, P.G. 8, 247. English text: ed. Al. Roberts, A.N.F. II, 209-298.

_______ *Stromata*, P.G. 8, 685, P.G. 9,9. English text: ed. Al. Roberts, A.N.F. II, 299-402; ed. also Otto Stählin (Leipzig: 1936).

Clement of Rome, *Epistola ad Corinthios*, P.G. 1, 201.

Cyril of Jerusalem, *Catechesis*, P.G. 33, 369-1125.

Didache, *Die Apostolischen Väter*, ed. K. Bihlmeyer, (Tübingen: 1924).

Didascalia Apostolorum, ed. Fr. X. Funk, (Torino: 1964.)

Dionysius Areopagita, *De Ecclesiastica Hierarchia*, P.G. 3, 585.

Dorotheus, Archimandrite, *Doctrina*, P.G. 88, 1632.

Ephraem Syrus, *Opera Omnia*, ed. J. S. Assemani, (Rome: 1732-1746).

Epiphanius of Cyprus, *Adversus Octoginta Haereses*, or *Panarion*, P.G. 41-42.

Eusebius of Caesarea, *Apologetica*, P.G. 21, 985.

_______ *Historia Ecclesiastica*, P.G. 20, 45.

Eusebius of Cesarea, *Ecclesiastic History, The Fathers of the*

Evagrius of Pontus, *De Oratione*, P.G. 79, 1165.

_______ *Capita Practica*, P.G. 40, 1220.

Gennadius, *Illustrius Men*, P.N.F. III, 359.

Gregory of Nazianzus, *Orationes*, P.G. 35, 366.

Gregory of Nyssa, *Oratio Catechetica*, P.G. 45, 9.

_______ *De Anima et Resurrectione Dialogus*, P.G. 46, 12.

_______ *In Psalmorum Inscriptiones*, P.G. 44, 432.

_______ *De Anima et Resurrectione Dialogus*, PG 46, 12.

_______ *In Psalmorum Inscriptiones*, PG 44, 432.

Hippolytus of Rome, *The Apostolic Tradition*, critical ed. Gr. Dix, (London: SPCK 1968).

Ignatius of Antioch, *Epistola ad Philadelphios*, P.G. 5, 661.

_______ *Letter to Polycarpus* and

_______ *Letter to Romans*, ed. K. Bihlmeyer. *Die Apostolischen Väter*, (Tübingen: 1924).

Isidorus of Pelusium, *Epistolarum Libri Quinque*, P.G. 78, 77.

Jerome, *Letters*, P.L. 22, 1070.

Illustrius Men, ed. Ph. Schaff, P.N.F., III, 359.

John Chrysostom, *On Vainglory and the Right Way for Parents to Bring Up their Children*, tr. M. Laistner in *Christianity and Pagan Culture*, (New York: Ithaca, 1951).

_______ *De Anna*, P.G. 54, 631.

John Chrysostom, *Homiliae in Matthaeum*, P.G. 57-58.

_______ *Homiliae in Genesium*, P.G. 53-54.

John Climacus, *Klimax (= Ladder), ed. Sophronius, (Athens:* Astir, 1970)

_______ *The Ladder of Divine Ascent*, tr. L. Moore, intr. M. Heppell, (London: Faber and Faber Ltd., 1959).

John of Damascus, *Exposition of the Orthodox Faith*, tr. S. Salmond, P.N.F. IX, 1-101.

John Moschus, *Patrum Spirituale*, PG 87, 2852.

Justin Martyr, Apologiae, P.G. 6, 328, ed. Al. Roberts, A.N.F. I, 163-193.

_______ % *Questiones et Responsiones ad Orthodoxos*, P.G. 6, 1249. Life of St. Daniel, *Life of St. Daniel*, tr. El. Dawes, See: *Three Byzantine Saints*, tr. El. Dawes, (Oxford: Blackwell, 1948).

Macarius the Egyptian, *Homilies*, (in Greek), V.H.P. XLII.

Maximus Confessor, *Quaestiones ad Thalassium*, P.G. 90, 840.

_______ *Capitum de Caritate*, P.G. 90, 950.

Nilus the Ascetic, *Oratio*, P.G. 79,696.

Origen, *De Oratione*, P.G. 11,528.

Pachomius, *Praecepta*, P.G. 40, 948-952.

_______ *Regulae*, V.H.P. XL, 113-128.

Palladius, *Historia Lausiaca*, P.G. 34, 1001, tr. C. Butler, *The Lausiac History of Palladius*, (Cambridge, 1898).

_______ *Historia Monachorum*, P.G. 34, 441.

Plato, *Law*, ed. E. B. England, (London: Longmans, 1921).

Sophronius of Jerusalem, *De Confessione*, P.G. 87, 3369

Socrates, *Historia Ecclesiastica*, P.G. 67, 29.

Sozomenus, *Historia Ecclesiastica*, P.G. 67, 844-1630.

Symeon Confessor, *Vita St. Anastasii*, P.G. 114, 773-810.

Symeon the New Theologian, *Theological Works, Philokalia*, III, 260.

Tertullian, *Apology* and on *Idolatry*, tr. S. Thelwall, A.N.F. III.

Theodore Lector, *Historia Ecclesiastica*, P.G. 86, 165.

Theodore of Studio, *Poenae Monachorum*, P.G. 99, 1756.

Theodoretus of Cyrus, *Historia Religiosa*, P.G. 82, 1283, *Varia*

Coptica, ed. and tr. W. Crum, (Aberdeen: University Press, 1939).

Varsanuphius and John, tr. D. Chitty, P. OR., Tom. 31, Fasc 3.

Vie d'Alexandre l'Acémète, P. OR., Tom. 6, Fasc 5, No. 30.

Vita Marinae, P.L. 73, 693.

Vita Pachomii, V.H.P., XL and XLI.

B. Secondary Sources

This list includes only the works chiefly consulted, and does not contain those to which only occasional reference has been made.

Armstrong, A.H., *The Cambridge History of Later Greek Thought and Early Mediaeval Philosophy*, (Cambridge: University Press, 1967).

Ayer, J., *A Source Book for Ancient Church History* (New York: Charles, 1948).

Bihlmeyer, K., *Die Apostolischen Väter* (Tübingen, 1924).

Bones, C., in Intr. to *The Life of St. Antony*, V.H.P. XL, (Athens: Apostolike Diakonia, 1970).

Brown, P., *The World of Late Antiquity*, (London: Thames and Hudson, 1971).

Campbell, M., *The Greek Fathers* (London: Charles Black, 1963).

Campenhausen, H. von., *The Fathers of the Greek Church* (London: Charles Black, 1963).

Cavarnos, C., *Byzantine Thought and Art*, (Belmont Mass: 1968)

Chadwick, O., *John Cassian*, (Cambridge University Press, 1968)

Chitty, D., *The Desert a City* (Oxford: Basil Blackwell, 1966).

Cochrane, Ch., *Christianity and Classical Culture* (New York: Oxford University Press, 1957).

Cruttwell, Ch., *A Literary History of Early Christianity*, II (London: Charles Black, 1893).

Daniélou, J., and H. Marrou, *The First Six Hundred Years*, 2 vols., tr. V. Cronin, (London: Longmans, 1964).

Dix, Gr., *The Treatise on the Apostolic Tradition of St. Hippolytus*, 2nd ed. (London: S.P.C.K., 1968).

Dobzhansky, Th., *Heredity and Nature of Man* (New York: Harcourt Brace, 1964).

Eby, F. and T. Arrowood, *History and Philosophy of Education* (Englewood Cliffs: Prentice-Hall, 1958).

Florovsky, G., "Empire and Desert" in *Greek Theological Review*, VI (New York, 1952).

Fortescue, Ad., *The Orthodox Eastern Church* (London: Catholic Truth Society, 1908).

Goodenough, Er., *The Church in the Roman Empire* (New York: Coore Square Publisher, 1970).

Graves, Fr., *A History of Education before the Middle Ages* (New York: MacMillan, 1916).

Hannay, J., *The Spirit and Origin of Christian Monasticism* (London: Methuen & Co., 1903).

Harnack, A.D. von., *Das Mönchthum, seine Ideal und seine Geschichte* (Giessen, 1881).

_______ *Monasticism and Confessions of St. Augustine*, tr. E. Kellett, (London: Williams and Morgate, 1901).

Hatch, Ed., *The Influence of Greek Ideas on Christianity* (New York: Harper Torch Books, 1957).

Haussic, H., *A History of Byzantine Civilization*, tr. J. Hussey (London: Thames and Hudson, 1971).

Hodgson, Ger., *Primitive Christian Education* (Edinburgh: Clarc, 1906).

Jaeger, W., *Two Rediscovered Works of Ancient Christian Literature:* Gregory of Nyssa and Macarius (Leiden: Brill, 1954)

_______ *Early Christianity and Greek Paideia* (Cambridge: Harvard University Press, 1961).

Kornarakes, J., *Paterika Biomata* (Salonika: 1971).

Koukoules, Ph., *Bios Byzantinon II* (Athens: 1948).

Lambros, Sp., "A Few Words Concerning Slavs in the Peloponnese," in *Hore*, May 5 (Greece: 1874).

Laister, M., *Christianity and Pagan Culture* (New York: Ithica, 1951).

Marique, P., *Early Christian Education* (New York: Fordham University Press, 1924.

Marrou, H., *A History of Education in Antiquity*, tr. G. Lamb (New York: Mentor, 1964).

Mastrogiannopoulos, El., *Hoi Pateres tes Ekklesias kai Ho Anthropos* (Athens: ZOE, 1966).

McCormick, P., *History of Education* (Washington: The Catholic Education Press, 1957).

Meyendorff, J., *Christ in Eastern Christian Thought* (N.York: St. Vladimir's Seminary Press, 1975).

Monroe, P., *A Text-Book in the History of Education* (New York: MacMillan Co., 1906).

Morrison, E., *St. Basil and His Rule* (London: Oxford University Press, 1912).

Mouratides, K., *Christokentrike Poimantike* (Athens: 1962).

Myers, Ed., *Education in the Perspective of History* (New York: Happer Bros., 1960).

Nigg, W., *Warriors of God*, tr. H. Ilford (London: Secker and Warburg, 1939).

O'Connor, J., *Monasticism and Civilization* (New York: Kenedy, 1921).

Paschos, P., *Gerontikon* (Athens: Astir, 1970).

Phytrakes, A., *Monks as Social Teachers* (in Greek), (Athens: Apostolike Diakonia, 1950).

Power, E., *Main Currents in the History of Education* (New York: McGraw-Hill, 1970).

Quasten, J., *Patrology*, vols. 1-3 (Utrecht: Spectrum Publishers, 1950-1960).

Ralles, G., and M. Potles, *Syntagma Hieron Canonon* (Athens: 1852-1859).

Sherrill, L., *The Rise of Christian Education* (New York: MacMillan Co., 1944).

Shiel, J., *Greek Thought and the Rise of Christianity* (London: Longmans, 1968).

Smith, I., *Rise of Christian Monasticism* (London: A. Innes, 1892).

Sumner, D., "St. John Climacus," in *The Guild of Pastoral Psychology*, Lecture 63 (London: 1950).

Vacalopoulos, A., *Origins of the Greek Nation*, tr. I. Moles (New Brunswick: Rutgers University Press, 1970).

Vööbus, A., *History of Asceticism in the Syrian Orient*, CSCO Subsidia, Tomus 17, (Louvain: 1960).

Waddell, H., *The Desert Fathers* (London: Constable Ltd., 1936).

Wallace-Hadrill, *Greek Patristic View of Nature* (New York: Barnes & Noble, 1968).

Woodhouse, F., *Monasticism: Ancient and Modern* (London: Gardner Darton, 1896).

Workman, B., *The Evolution of Monastic Ideals* (London: Charles H. Kelly, 1913).

Bibliographical Note:

For further study the following works are suggested.

I. *The Life of St. Antony.* A very important document for the study of the early monasticism. It was composed in 357 A.D. by St. Athanasius, the bishop of Alexandria. It has been translated into English by K. T. Meyer (Ancient Christian Writers 10; Westminster, Md.:1950).

II. *The Lausiac History of Palladius.* Palladius reports in his history, composed in 419/420, what he saw and heard during the twelve years he spent with the hermits in the Egyptian desert. He is one of the most outstanding historians of early monasticism. An English translation of *The Lausiac History* has been made by W. Clark (London: 1918).

III. *Apophthegmata.* This is an anonymous collection of spiritual "sayings" of the Desert Fathers compiled around the end of the fifth century. It is of great value since it gives a clear idea of the spirit of the Egyptian monasticism. H. Waddell has translated the *Apophthegmata* from the Latin version into English under the title *The Desert Fathers* (Ann Arbor: Ann Arbor Paperbacks, 1966).